Helion & Company Limited
26 Willow Road
Solihull
West Midlands
B91 1UE
England
Tel. 0121 705 3393
Fax 0121 711 4075
email: info@helion.co.uk
website: www.helion.co.uk
Twitter: @helionbooks
Visit our blog http://blog.helion.co.uk

Published by Helion & Company 2017
Designed and typeset by Farr out
    Publications, Wokingham, Berkshire
Cover designed by Paul Hewitt, Battlefield
    Design (www.battlefield-design.co.uk)
Printed by Henry Ling Limited, Dorchester,
    Dorset

Text © Santiago Rivas 2016
Illustrations © Santiago Rivas unless
    otherwise noted

ISBN 978-1-911096-02-3

British Library Cataloguing-in-Publication
    Data
A catalogue record for this book is available
    from the British Library

All rights reserved. No part of this
publication may be reproduced, stored,
manipulated in any retrieval system, or
transmitted in any mechanical, electronic
form or by any other means, without the
prior written authority of the publishers,
except for short extracts in media
reviews. Any person who engages in any
unauthorised activity in relation to this
publication shall be liable to criminal
prosecution and claims for civil and criminal
damages.

For details of other military history titles
published by Helion & Company Limited
contact the above address, or visit our
website: http://www.helion.co.uk

We always welcome receiving book
proposals from prospective authors working
in military history.

CONTENTS

FOREWORD

By General Rafael del Pino (Pilot of the Fuerza Aérea Revolucionaria during the fight over Playa Girón)

When historian Santiago Rivas contacted me in mid-2014 to know more about the Bay of Pigs invasion organized by the United States government in April 1961, I offered him my full co-operation regarding the experiences living through that transcendental episode of the Cuban Revolution. What I never imagined was that young Santiago would make a research work so thorough, deep and, doubtless, impressive.

More than half a century has passed since that battle, and the different memories of the protagonists, together with the years that have passed and the logical effects of age, have made it very hard to reconcile what happened at the same time on both sides, a difficulty that Santiago Rivas has masterfully managed to overcome, with extraordinary patience and dedication.

My congratulations to Santiago for his great work. Historians, and especially lovers of aviation, have in this work a priceless guide to understanding one of the primary events that contributed to consolidating the Cuban Revolution in the middle of the last century.

INTRODUCTION

The Cuban exiles' invasion at Bay of Pigs in April 1961 is a clear example of a poorly planned and executed military operation, which became one of the biggest military failures of the Western powers in their fight against communism during the Cold War years. The need by the United States government for "plausible deniability" of their involvement and lack of decision by the Kennedy administration were among the main causes of the disaster.

The invasion, planned by the US government through the Central Intelligence Agency (CIA), had the intention of overthrowing the government headed by Fidel Castro Ruz, who, after defeating the forces of Cuban dictator Fulgencio Batista on 1 January 1959, was ruling the country and driving it towards communism. Despite Castro counting initially as a neutral, or even having some support from the US government, the threat felt by the latter on their interests on Cuba and the lobby made by some exiles of the former government and local politicians, led the US to a position opposing Castro.

The US and Cuban positions went in different directions and towards a more aggressive confrontation during the two years from the triumph of the revolution until US President John F. Kennedy approved the invasion.

A series of failures - from the decision to choose an intelligence agency with no war experience to conduct the direction of the invasion, to the space given to some of the most hated people of the Batista regime in the highest positions of the invasion force, the decision not to give enough support to the groups already fighting Castro in Cuba and the plan to make a conventional invasion instead of placing guerrilla forces across the country - led to the disaster at Girón Beach on Bay of Pigs, where on 20 April the last forces surrendered, with only few managing to escape.

The Cuban revolutionary forces managed to defeat the invasion with an unprepared army, organized with some of the forces remaining from the Batista era and veterans of the revolution forces, together with militias organized since 1959 to fight the expected invasion.

The newly created Fuerza Aérea Revolucionaria (FAR, Revolutionary Air Force) played a vital role, destroying some of the most important landing and support ships and shooting down part of the aggressor's air force. The FAR was equipped with B-26 Invader light bombers, a few transport aircraft,. Hawker Sea Furies and Lockheed T-33s, but despite many of their aircraft being in poor condition, and having fewer pilots, they still managed to rule the air space over the area of operations.

The defeat of the invasion, in which the US government tried not to be involved but in the end had to recognize its participation, led to the consolidation of Castro's power and a tighter turn towards communism, culminating a year later with the Cuban Missile Crisis, when the Soviet Union attempted to install nuclear missiles on the island to threaten the USA. The invasion's failure also led to the exiles being less optimistic about the possibility of overthrowing Castro and the end of US support for a military solution. In the end, the communist government continued to rule Cuba, as it still does today, 66 years after the revolution seized power and 26 years after the ending of support by the Soviet Union.

The Cuban government, aware of the threat posed by the exiles, worked hard after the invasion on the reinforcement of its armed forces, something that had already started before the Bay of Pigs events, with strong Soviet support. MiG-15s and 19s replaced the old Sea Furies and T-33s, later followed by MiG-17s and 21s, creating one of the most powerful Latin American Air Forces. The Revolutionary Army also received a big boost with tanks, artillery and light weapons, while training was performed in the Soviet Union, China and other communist bloc countries, leaving no possibility of success for a new invasion attempt.

CHAPTER 1
FROM INDEPENDENCE TO REVOLUTION

Cuba, being one of the first islands discovered by Christopher Columbus, was a very important place for the Spanish colonies in Latin America, with La Habana harbour a bastion of royalist forces during the independence wars.

Independence movements began late on the island, backed by the US, especially, the southern states, who wanted to annex Cuba as a slave state, because the black people there outnumbered the white. Three revolts occurred in 1848, 1850 and 1851, headed by former Spanish Army General Narciso López, all backed by the US, but after the Confederate States lost the American Civil War and slavery was abolished, such schemes were abandoned.

However, the revolts and what had happened elsewhere in the Americas led to growing independence sentiments among the Cuban people, and the Liberals rose up against Spanish rule in 1968, headed by Carlos Manuel de Céspedes, leading to a 10-year-long civil war which ended in the defeat of the rebels. But the Spanish government agreed to sign the Pact of Zanjón, whereby it compromised to make some reforms to give more freedom to the islanders. Slavery was finally abolished in 1886, but as the planned reforms were not made, in 1879 José Martí and Tomás Estrada Palma had begun a new revolt, which ended a year later with their defeat. Yet the independence flame was afire, and in 1895 the final independence war began, headed by Antonio Maceo and Máximo Gómez as the military heads, with José Martí as the ideologue. The latter was killed at the Battle of Dos Ríos on 19 May 1895, and Maceo died at Punta Brava on 7 December 1896. The Spanish sent a major reinforcement to the island, changing the tide of the war against the Cubans, but the US government became interested in forcing the Spanish from the island and used the pretext of the destruction of the USS *Maine* battleship in La Habana harbour on 15 February 1898 to declare war on Spain.

Shortly after, on 12 August, Spanish forces surrendered and the island was occupied by the US on 1 January 1899, as soon as the last Spanish combatants left the island. General John R. Brooke was appointed governor of the island, creating the Rural Guard and municipal police forces, these being Cuba's first local security forces.

Despite the US government being keen on the possibility of annexing Cuba, the pressure on the island for independence led to an assurance that the occupation was temporary, and in 1902 Tomás Estrada Palma was elected as the first president of the Cuban Republic (he was the sole candidate on the elections).

Despite this, Cuba did not have total independence, as the US government's Platt Amendment limited the freedom of the country. This document stated that Cuba could not transfer Cuban land to any power other than the United States. Cuba could contract no foreign debt without guarantees that the interest could be served from ordinary revenues. The US government kept the right of intervention in Cuban affairs, and of military occupation if it considered that the life, property or rights of US citizens were in danger. Cuba was prohibited from negotiating treaties with any country other than the United States "which will impair or to impair the independence of Cuba". The Cubans were also prohibited to "permit any foreign power or powers to obtain … lodgment in or control over any portion" of Cuba. The Isla de Pinos (now the Isla de la Juventud) was deemed outside the boundaries of Cuba until the title to it was adjusted in a future treaty (Cuban sovereignty over the island was finally recognized in 1925). The sale or lease to the United States of "lands necessary for coaling or naval stations at certain specified points" were to be agreed upon. Finally, the amendment ceded to the United States the Cuban naval base at Guantánamo Bay and granted the right to use a number of other naval bases as coal stations.

This amendment was in force until 1934, but the country remained under US influence for much longer.

Remains of the USS *Maine* at La Habana, destroyed on 15 February 1898.

The Cuartel Moncada, which Castro and other rebels attempted to capture on 26 July 1953, after the failed attack.

One of the eight Marmon-Herrington CTMS 1TB1 light tanks acquired by Cuba.

One of the 15 Cuban Comet tanks.

Internal struggle continued in the meantime, and Estrada Palma faced a new revolt in 1906. He asked for US intervention, which led in September to a new occupation that lasted until February 1909, after José Miguel Gómez had became the new president in November 1908.

A period of relative stability followed, but there were still flashpoints, including some US intervention to protect their interests on the sugar plantations. President Gerardo Machado, elected in 1925, changed the constitution to be re-elected, starting a period of increasing corruption and instability, but in September 1933 he was forced to resign when he lost the support of the armed forces during a general strike.

The rise of Fulgencio Batista
Ramón Grau de San Martín became provisional president and performed many political changes to the country, but he was overthrown in January 1934 by a new rebellion backed by the USA and led by Army Sergeant Fulgencio Batista.

A dark period then began in Cuba, with political instability, in which the country had three presidents in the following two years, while the real power was in the hands of Batista, who became the head of the Army. Batista ruled with an iron hand and suppressed all strikes or protests against the government.

After elections in 1936, Miguel Mariano Gómez assumed the presidency, but he was forced to resign before the year end, the government left in the hands of his vice-president, Federico Laredo Bru, until 1940.

In that year, Batista was elected as president, making some economic changes to the country, while in 1941, after the attack on Pearl Harbor, he declared war on the Axis powers, supporting the USA. In 1944, he left the government to Grau de San Martín and went to live to Florida, returning in 1948.

Grau de San Martín governed during a period of economic growth, thanks to the rise of the price of sugar, but corruption also grew in an already unequal society, where power was concentrated in a few people. He was followed in 1948 by Carlos Prío Socarrás, with Batista elected senator, but instability in the country was growing at the same time as corruption and persecution of political opponents.

Despite elections being planned for 1952, a coup d'état headed by Batista on 10 March brought him back to power, suppressing most of the country's liberties and starting a bloody dictatorship, which led to the formation of groups opposing the government.

The years of revolution
Opposition to the government began to grow and new organizations were formed. One of them, with 164 men headed by young lawyer Fidel Castro Ruz, attempted on 26 July 1953 to seize the Moncada and Carlos Manuel de Céspedes barracks, the first at Santiago de Cuba and the other at Bayamo, with the intention of capturing weapons and broadcasting a declaration of an uprising against the government, using the radio stations at the barracks. Both attacks failed and most of the attackers were captured, 65 of them being killed by Army forces despite them having surrendered. Fidel Castro, his brother Raúl and other revolutionaries were jailed after an Army officer refused to obey an order to kill them. They were sentenced to 15 years in prison, but two years later they were freed on the condition that they leave Cuba.

Before leaving the country, Castro started to organize an underground movement headed by Frank País. He then went to Mexico, where he organized the Movimiento 26 de Julio, with the intention of returning to Cuba and starting guerrilla operations against the government. In Mexico, he met Argentine doctor Ernesto "Che" Guevara, who joined the rebels and would became one of the heads of the movement.

With the support of Cuban exiles living in the United States and the

Comet tanks in a parade at La Habana.

The *Granma* yacht used by the rebels to travel from Mexico to Cuba in 1957.

Fulgencio Batista, the dictator of Cuba, against whom the Movimiento 26 de Julio fought.

training of former Spanish Republican Army Colonel Alberto Bayo, the organization prepared to travel back to Cuba on the yacht *Granma*.

Meanwhile, Batista had called elections in 1954, but as the opposition left the process, he was elected president again, continuing with his oppressive government, which became more aggressive due to the activities of the revolutionaries.

On 2 December 1956, a group of 82 men of the Movimiento 26 de Julio landed from the *Granma* on the south of Cuba. Three days later, they were found by the Cuban Army and defeated at Alegría de Pío, 21 of the revolutionaries being killed and 26 captured. Only 17 survivors escaped, with almost no equipment or weapons, to the Sierra Maestra, where they started guerrilla operations.

The Batista government initially paid little interest in them, but many people, unhappy with the government, joined the rebels.

Discontent with the government grew, and on 5 September 1957 a group of naval officers organized a coup with the support of Army and Army Aviation personnel. Despite most of the organizers attempting to postpone the coup, the naval unit at Cayo Loco, in the city of Cienfuegos, was not informed and took action. They gained local support from civilians, but the government sent a column of troops and the unit had to surrender the next morning. However, some 100 men managed to escape to the nearby Escambray mountains, in the centre of the island, where they opened a second guerrilla front, called the Segundo Frente Nacional del Escambray. Another front was opened with about 100 men at Cordillera de los Órganos in Pinar del Río province, at the western end of the country. In the Sierra Maestra,

Rebels marching to La Habana on board a captured Sherman tank, on 1 January 1959.

Fidel Castro and other rebels entering La Habana after the victory of the revolution.

by the beginning of 1958, there were about 900 men involved in guerrilla operations.

The triumph of the revolution

The Batista regime became weaker, and on 18 March 1958, the US government declared an arms embargo, showing it was no longer supporting the dictator. In the meantime, Castro's forces declared a general strike on 9 April, while Raúl Castro went to the Sierra del Cristal, just to the north of the Sierra Maestra, in Holguín province.

The weakening of Batista's position led him to call for elections to be held in June, later rescheduled for November, but Castro's guerrillas opposed these moves, considering them a farce.

An Army offensive which started in May finished on the 25th of that month with the withdrawal of forces from the Sierra Maestra without achieving success.

A new offensive by the Army and Marines in July ended with the commander of one Marine battalion joining the guerrillas with part of his force, including a huge quantity of equipment. Army forces, meanwhile, made little progress, and August's rainy season forced them to retreat.

This easing of pressure made possible the creation of a column led by Ernesto "Che" Guevara, which started a march in the Escambray mountains, while another column, led by Camilo Cienfuegos, went to Yaguajay in Las Villas province (now Sancti Spiritus). These columns reached their area of operations by mid-October, by which time the guerrillas had grown in strength to about 7,000 men in four provinces.

The Batista forces were retreating and losing their will to fight, staying most of the time in their barracks, while the guerrillas increased their actions and control of the country. Finally, on 17 November, the guerrillas began a general offensive, leaving the Sierra

Fidel Castro during his first visit to the United States after the triumph of the revolution, in 1959.

Maestra and seizing the town of Bueycito, followed by Guisa and then Jiguani, cutting the central highway. By the end of the month, the cities of Santiago de Cuba and Guantanamo were encircled and most of the eastern part of the country was controlled by the guerrillas. The columns of Guevara and Cienfuegos then entered the action in the centre of the country, capturing most of the cities in the area.

On 29 December, Guevara's forces began an attack on the city of Santa Clara, where they fought a major battle against government forces, but the latter had almost no will to fight. In the meantime, the Batista regime was falling into pieces, and on 1 January 1959 he fled with his family to the Dominican Republic at the same time that the forces in Santa Clara were surrendering.

Castro and his forces started a march to La Habana, to prevent the Army or conservative sectors of the Cuban society from taking control of the government.

Finally, on 8 January, Castro made his triumphant entry into the city.

CHAPTER 2
FROM REVOLUTION TO INVASION

Just before Castro arrived in La Habana, politician Manuel Urrutia was named president on 3 January and appointed José Miró Cardona as prime minister two days later, with the intention of organizing a moderate transitional government. He appointed Fidel Castro as commander-in-chief of the armed forces, and on 5 January his government was recognized by the US.

As Urrutia opposed some of the socialist ideas of Castro, he resigned on 17 July and was replaced by communist lawyer Osvaldo Dorticós Torrado; but the real power was in the hands of Castro,

despite Dorticós remaining as president until 1976.

Huge reforms

One of the causes of Cuba's social problems was the situation created by the relationship with the US. Since independence was reached, the island had functioned as a dependent territory of the United States, with the government being manipulated by Washington through the State Department and their embassy in La Habana. Sugar production, which was one of the main economic resources of the island, was

A Cubana de Aviación Vickers Viscount, like those that defected to Miami on 26 April and 2 October 1959.

The cargo ship *La Coubre*, which exploded in La Habana harbour when she was carrying weapons for the Cuban Armed Forces. Castro's government accused the US and the exiles of causing the explosion.

in a large part in the hands of US companies, while most of the production was exported to the US. Also, tourism, another of the big income sources of the island, was in the hands of US companies. Gangsters, gamblers and prostitutes filled the casinos, while their owners were very close to the corrupt Cuban oligarchy. This led to an anti-American sentiment among the middle and lower classes, which saw them as the source of corruption in Cuba and most of the country's problems. This was aggravated by support for Batista from the Eisenhower administration.

Despite the US government initially trying to show support for the new government by recognizing it, it was clear that the social changes that Castro's forces wanted to perform would be against most of the US interests on the island.

What Castro had in mind was not only to overthrow Batista and end the dictatorship by starting a democracy; he wanted a deeper change in the country, including all social and economic aspects of life, as well as keeping power as long as possible. To keep the people on his side and justify fighting anyone who was against his changes, he needed a new enemy, and he found it in the United States.

The support for Batista was followed by US acceptance of the activities of former Batista followers, who immediately after their defeat began to plot against Castro from Florida. They would soon be joined by many people who were in favour of a more moderate government after the revolution and were disenchanted by Castro's rule.

It is interesting to note that the Cuban Communist Party did not support Castro, who wasn't considered a communist. After his triumph, he started turning to the left, but didn't declare himself as a communist until 16 April 1961, the day after the bombing by the counter-revolutionary forces prior to the Bay of Pigs invasion.

Immediately after the success of the revolution, the rebels started to prosecute supporters of the Batista regime, first those more related to the persecution of dissidents, but later everyone involved with the government and in the end, all those accused of not being in favour of the revolution. Despite in many cases there not being much evidence, almost everyone tried was jailed, and hundreds were executed under the supervision of Ernesto "Ché" Guevara.

Guevara, a passionate communist, was one of the ideologues of the turn to communism by the revolution and the leaving behind of moderates. He also boosted the ideas of cleansing the armed forces of former Batista supporters and everyone not implicated with the revolution. Guevara, together with Raúl Castro and other revolutionaries, were working secretly, with Fidel, with reforms to establish a socialist country. This group was becoming the real power

behind the scenes, and their ideas become evident when, on 7 May, they sanctioned agrarian reform and Guevara became the head of the Agrarian Reform Institute, which started to expropriate land in the hands of the big landowners, some of them US citizens.

On 10 January 1959, the Cuban government started diplomatic relations with the Soviet Union, one day after they legalized the Communist Party in the country.

A request by the Cuban government for the US to return former Batista supporters who went into exile in America was ignored, giving Castro another reason to accuse the US of supporting Batista. Despite Castro knowing they couldn't be deported by the US government, because the revolutionaries were not following a standard procedure to judge them, the US could have prevented the exiles from plotting against the revolution and even carrying out sabotage operations from US territory or smuggling weapons to anti-Castro activists in Cuba.

On 24 March, Fidel Castro stated for the first time that a counter-revolution was being planned in the US by the exiles, with the support of the US; at the same time, a Batista organization called Rosa Blanca (White Rose) began operations in Miami, without the US government doing anything to prevent it.

After a visit to Venezuela, from 25-27 April, Castro visited the United States and met vice-president Richard Nixon, but was not received by Eisenhower. He was treated as a revolutionary and a supporter of democracy during his visit.

The growth of communism among the revolutionary government was becoming evident. On 29 June, the head of the recently created Fuerza Aérea FAR, (Revolutionary Air Force), Major Pedro Luis Díaz Lanz, who was one of the main pilots who helped the rebels by sending weapons to the Sierra Maestra, was removed from his position. On 1 July, he fled the island and informed the US Senate Internal Security Subcommittee that the communists were taking over the island.

Diaz Lanz's declarations were used by Castro to state that the US government was involved in anti-revolution activities and led to the removal of president Urrutia and the appointment of Dorticós in his place, in a clear sign for the moderates that the communists were gaining power.

The selection of Dorticós by the leaders of the revolution, in spite of there being a democratic process available, was explained by a statement by Castro that with such a powerful enemy as the United States, the revolution could not afford the luxury of such a process. In the meantime, he used the accusations of communism against the revolution as a weapon to equate anti-communism with counter-revolution, thus eliminating from the government all those who were not communists and starting to fight everyone in the country who was against communism.

Anti-revolutionary activities

As soon as the revolution succeeded, organizations to fight it were born, initially with Batista supporters who wanted a return to the

A DC-3 of Aerovías Q. A Curtiss C-46 of the company defected to the US on 15 April 1959.

previous status quo. The first organization was the Rosa Blanca, but most of its members had fled to the United States and had little contact with Cuba.

On 2 February 1959, US citizen Alleu Robert Meller was arrested after he entered Cuba on a small plane with the intention of killing Fidel Castro, being the first action against his regime. This action was followed by others during the year, including the hijacking of a Curtiss C-46 of Aerovías Q on 15 April and a Vickers Viscount of Cubana de Aviación airline over Varadero, which was redirected to Miami on 26 April. On 14 June, a Douglas DC-3 of the Revolutionary Air Force, flying from La Habana to Camagüey, was deflected to Miami by four officers who were against the revolution.

Sabotage operations and attacks against members of the government started to rise and, as the differences with the US government also grew, the participation of the US government was also increased. On 8 August, Stanley F. Vesson, from the US Embassy in La Habana, was arrested while going to a meeting with anti-revolutionary organizations.

Five days later, a Curtiss C-46 from the Dominican Republic was captured at Trinidad Airport, in Las Villas province, while carrying 10 people and weapons for the counter-revolutionaries. This operation had been backed by the Dominican dictator Rafael Trujillo and was part of an invasion planned to overrun Castro.

On 2 October, another Viscount of Cubana de Aviación was redirected to Miami by people who were escaping the revolution.

Counter-revolutionary groups began to operate from the United States, from where they supported the activities on the island, using boats and planes to carry men and weapons, and dropping incendiary bombs on sugar cane fields. The activities of small planes all over Cuba led to a protest, on 6 October, by the Cuban government to the US State Department, as the planes were coming to the island from the US.

Four days later, another plane of Cubana de Aviación was hijacked and forced to land in Miami, while on the following day a small airplane dropped incendiary bombs on the Central Niágara sugar mill, in Pinar del Río province, and on 13 October, another plane did the same at the Central Punta Alegre mill in Camagüey. This attack was repeated six days later.

Politically, the country was moving further from the United States, while the communist were gaining power every day. One of the reasons for this was the lack of action by the US government against the exiles who were starting to operate against the revolution. On 22 October, while Castro was meeting at the La Habana Hilton with members of the American Society of Travel Agents, Major Díaz Lanz appeared over the city in a B-25 Mitchell bomber dropping leaflets against the communist infiltration in Cuba. Cuban troops opened fire on the plane with machine guns, but instead of shooting it down their fire caused 42 wounded and four dead in the city. On the same day, a small plane strafed a train in Las Villas province, and six days later, the sugar plantations at Niágara and Violete (in Camagüey province) were again attacked with incendiary bombs.

Castro's reaction was to accuse the US government of supporting such actions, as it was not possible that they could not control their own airfields. On the same day as the raid of Díaz Lanz, Castro had arrested Major Huber Matos, one of the main leaders of the revolution and now commander of Camagüey province, because he resigned from the Revolutionary Army in protest against the communist infiltration. Castro accused him of treason, equating his actions with anti-communism, and he was sentenced to 20 years in prison (he was released in 1979 and exiled, dying in Miami in February 2014), despite Guevara and Raúl Castro wanting to execute him.

A government purge followed in November 1959, with all moderates removed, leaving room for the extremists in the final turn towards communism.

US property also started to be taken over, starting with cattle land of the King Ranch Company at Camagüey.

Three more air attacks with incendiary bombs took place on 4 November in Oriente province.

During the year, several organizations were created inside Cuba to fight the now communist-oriented revolution, the most important being the Movimiento de Recuperación Revolucionaria (MRR), Directorio Revolucionario Estudiantil (DRE), Movimiento Revolucionario del Pueblo (MRP) and Movimiento 30 de Noviembre.

Enter the CIA

By the end of 1959, the CIA began to make contact with the MRR and DRE, formed by former members of the Movimiento 26 de Julio and some Batista supporters. In the meantime, Cuba reached a deal with the Soviet Union to sell them sugar in exchange for providing oil for the island.

Early in 1960, some organizations began guerrilla activities in the Escambray hills, in the southern central section of the island, while the CIA started to work with the intention of merging the disparate groups, creating the Frente Revolucionario Democrático, an organization to co-ordinate the operations of about a dozen counter-revolutionary groups.

The United States began to take its first measures against the Cuban government, announcing on 26 May that all existing aid programmes to Cuba had been cancelled. Then, on 5 July, after the continuous expropriation of US-owned properties on the island, President Eisenhower decided to withdraw all the Cuban sugar quota for the balance of the year, which meant the end of US sugar purchases from the island.

Rebel activities against the Cuban government continued, with an attack at La Habana province on 12 January, when a plane dropped incendiary bombs, followed by other attacks on 18, 28 and 30 January in La Habana, Matanzas Camagüey and Oriente provinces. On 21 January, a plane dropped four 50kg bombs over the towns of Regla and Cojímar at La Habana, and on 7 February, a plane dropped incendiary bombs at the Estrella, Céspedes, Florida and Violeta sugar plantations and destroyed 16,500 tons of sugar cane. Central España was then bombed on 18 February, but one bomb exploded before being released and the plane crashed, killing the pilot, US citizen Robert Ellis Frost. Incendiary attacks continued on 23 February at Washington Mill in Las Villas and Ulacia in Matanzas.

However, the most significant action occurred on 4 March, when, while unloading a major weapons cargo purchased in Belgium, the French cargo ship La Coubre exploded in La Habana harbour, killing more than 100 and wounding 200, as well as causing the loss of the cargo and almost destroying the ship. Castro accused the counter-revolutionaries and US government of this attack, but it was never proved if it was an accident or a terrorist act.

The operation of planes coming from the United States, mainly against sugar cane plantations, continued on 8 March at San Cristóbal, Pinar del Río province, and on 4 April at Buey Cabón, Oriente province.

After a short time in which the war consisted mainly of the words and actions of the US and Cuban governments, and with the increasing activities of counter-revolutionary organizations - mainly in the Escambray area - on 28 September 1960, a Bristol Britannia flying from La Habana to Madrid was hijacked by exiles, while the Piper Super Cruiser serialled CU-E-310 was also hijacked and flew to Florida with other exiles.

On the following day, a DC-4 dropped a major cargo of weapons on the Escambray area, followed on 8 October by another plane on

On 8 December 1959, a DC-3 of Cubana de Aviación was attempted to be hijacked while flying from Santiago de Cuba to La Habana, but the pilot managed to frustrate the action, despite later dying from wounds suffered during the attempt.

On 11 March 1960, Rafael del Pino took off on the T-33, serialled FAR-709, to intercept an AT-11 that was close to Mariel Naval Air Base. After a first strafing attack, he saw the plane making a belly landing in the sea. The plane and crew were never found by the Cubans.

the same mission.

The hijacking or stealing of planes to fly into exile continued during the year. On 14 October, three Aeroncas (serials CU-E-596, CU-E-731 and CU-E-723), two Pipers (CU-E-596 and 589) and one Cessna 170 (CU-E-552) were flown to the United States, while on 29 October, a DC-3 was siezed and forced to fly to Key West. During the latter action, a soldier was killed and the pilot and a 14-year-old passenger were injured.

A Piper (serial CU-E-4441) was also taken to the United States on 29 November, and on 8 December, another DC-3 of Cubana de Aviación was subject to an attempted hijacking while flying from Santiago de Cuba to La Habana, but the pilot managed to frustrate the action, despite later dying from wounds he received in the incident.

Sabotage operations against the government and the now government-controlled media grew all over the country, while in the Escambray hills the guerrilla organizations kept fighting against the poorly trained Milicias Revolucionarias and Ejército Revolucionario.

Before the end of the year, the Luscombe 8E serialled CU-E-310 and the Antonov An-2 CU-E-797 were taken to the United States by exiles.

From the second half of 1960 until the Girón invasion, the attacks by planes on sugar plantations ceased, as their operations were focused on dropping weapons to the rebels in the Escambray area and dropping pamphlets, mostly by night.

Sabotage operations had destroyed about 300,000 tons of sugar cane in around 800 fires; they had also caused about 150 other fires and were involved in 110 bombings, derailing six trains and damaging the Santiago de Cuba oil refinery, leaving it out of action for a week.

In the meantime, as the operations at Escambray were increasing, in December 1960 the Cuban government decided to organize a huge operation against the rebels, mobilizing about 60,000 men of the Army and Milicias Revolucionarias to the area.

The operation was to annihilate the guerrillas, who consisted of less than 1,000 men. The operations across the hills began on 1 January 1961 and led to many actions against the rebels, including combats at Arroyo Malo, Jorobada and San Ambrosio, until by mid-March the rebels were completely disorganized and numbered no more than 200 men, with most of their leaders captured or killed. The groups had, however, gained experience and were reorganized to keep fighting.

During this time, on 9 January 1961, a Cessna 310 serialled FAR-53 of the Fuerza Aérea Revolucionaria was shot down by mistake by the men of the Milicias Revolucionarias while attempting to land at Varadero, when it was confused for a plane of the counter-revolutionaries.

As operations by planes coming from the US to drop weapons or pamphlets continued, shortly after 6:00 p.m. on 11 March, a Beechcraft AT-11 with US serial N-150 or N-156 was detected flying to the west of La Habana. The alert was sent to San Antonio de los Baños Air Base and the Lockheed T-33 serialled FAR-709, with pilot Rafael del Pino, was scrambled to intercept it. Del Pino took off and headed to Mariel Air Base (which had belonged to the now disbanded Naval Aviation), 50km to the west of La Habana, and from there turned north. After making several circles about 70km from the coast, he descended to 1,000ft and started to return when he saw a silver dot to his right leaving the island over Baracoa Beach. He informed the tower and went to inspect the plane, starting to circle over it. Del Pino received an order to force it to land or shoot it down, and after some passes trying unsuccessfully to make it change course, he decided to attack. On a first pass, as the AT-11 was flying very slowly, he couldn't track the plane in his sights, so he went for a second pass, but lost sight of the plane briefly. Then he saw it to his left and descended upon it, managed to put the plane in his sights and opened fire. He passed the plane very closely, and when he turned for a new attack he saw the plane descending fast and flying very low for some seconds, before making a belly landing on the sea, despite Del Pino not managing to hit the AT-11. He kept flying over the plane, watching as the two crew members inflated a life-raft and escaped, and asked for a rescue helicopter or a Consolidated Catalina, but they were not available and night was coming. Del Pino returned to his base and no trace was ever found of the AT-11 or its crew.

This was the only interception of a plane supporting the rebels before the Bay of Pigs invasion, but activities by planes flying from the United States to carry weapons, drop pamphlets or on reconnaissance flights continued. Reports received by the Cuban government included a flight of jet aircraft, most probably US Air Force reconnaissance planes, as by then USAF Lockheed U-2 and RF-101 Voodoos were performing reconnaissance flights over the island.

On one occasion, FAR pilot Álvaro Prendes took off in the T-33 serialled FAR-709 to try to intercept a jet flying very high over San Antonio de los Baños, whose contrail was seen from the base. At 30,000ft, he managed to get close to the plane, which, according to Prendes, was an F-86 Sabre, but in fact was an RF-101 Voodoo, and fired his machine guns, but the US plane was faster and escaped.

On 20 March 1961, the Cubans knew that an invasion was imminent, and as a radio was broadcasting against the Castro government from Swan Island, near the coast of Honduras, a C-46 was sent with pilots Toti Foyo and Fernando Álvarez, escorted by two T-33 flown by Enrique Carreras Rolas and Rafael del Pino, to make a reconnaissance of the island and check if there were rebel forces being assembled there. The island has a small runway, so it was possible that combat planes could be based there. As the island was 350 miles from Cuba, the T-33 had to wait for the C-46 closer to Cuba, to protect it on its return. The C-46 took off at 12:15 p.m., with the T-33 of Carreras taking off 40 minutes later and the plane of Del Pino at 1.10 p.m. When the T-33s were close to the island, Carreras broke radio silence to inform Del Pino that they would continue flying to the island, instead of waiting 25 miles away, keeping to a height of 25,000ft. Over the island, Carreras saw the C-46 making a first pass over the runway, leading to a general alert of the small garrison, which immediately started to put fuel tanks on the runway to block any landing attempt. On a second pass, the crew of the C-46 took some pictures and started to return, while Del Pino stayed for 10 minutes to check that no plane was following the C-46. The planes returned to Cuba without trouble, but Del Pino had to land at San Julián airfield, on the west of Cuba, because clouds forced him to change course and he was running out of fuel.

This was one of two reconnaissance missions before the invasion performed by the FAR. The second was performed around this time over Grand Cayman, with a single B-26, which flew over the airport and returned, seeing nothing unusual.

CHAPTER 3
BRIGADE 2506

After the successful operation organized by the CIA to overthrow Guatemalan president Jacobo Arbenz in 1954, putting Colonel Carlos Castillo Armas in power, US President Dwight D. Eisenhower was convinced that the same could be done in Cuba, helping to form a force of exiles to destroy Castro's forces.

The original plan was to form small infiltration teams, with radio operators and sabotage experts to join the local guerrilas. This later evolved into a force of about 500 trained men that could join those forces fighting the revolution inside Cuba, preparing them to be a bigger threat to government forces.

On 17 March 1960, Eisenhower ordered the CIA Director, Allen Dulles, to start the preparation of the Cuban exiles force, while a government-in-exile had to be organized to become the leadership of

the exiles and legitimize their army. Under the plan, called "A Program of Covert Action Against the Castro Regime", the CIA began to make contact with the exiles in Miami, where most of them had gone to live, creating a town called Little La Habana. The CIA wanted the exiles army to include more of the rightist exiles, most of them former Batista supporters, and giving less space to left-of-centre groups, which included some former Movimiento 26 de Julio veterans.

This angered some exiles, who saw some questionable former Bastista supporters among the leaders of the new army. The Frente Revolucionario Democrático (FRD) was created in May, with a leadership of exiles, to perform resistance activities inside Cuba and also co-ordinate operations from the US. Dr Manuel Artime, head of the Movimiento de Recuperación Revolucionaria (MRR) and a

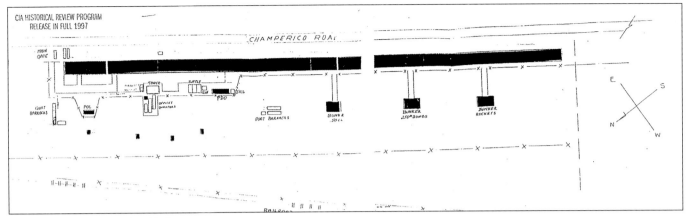

Diagram of Base Rayo at Retalhuleu.

former member of the Movimiento 26 de Julio, was its leader, together with Manuel Antonio de Varona, José Ignacio Rasco, Dr Justo Carrillo Hernández and Aureliano Sánchez Arango.

Training of the first 28 recruited fighters began in June 1960 at Useppa Island, close to Fort Myers in Florida, from where they were moved to the Jungle Warfare Training Center at Fort Guilick, in the Panama Canal Zone, while some recruits were initially trained in Louisiana, Texas and Virginia. They would become the leaders of the exile army and help in the training of other troops. A CIA agent, with the cover name of Frank Bender (code name for Jerry Droller), was chosen to take charge of the training, having experience with the French Maquis in the Second World War, but with no knowledge of Latin America or even of the Spanish language, something that would be one of the main problems in the organization of this new force.

Cuban head of the exile army was José "Pepe" Peréz San Román, a former Cuban Army officer who had undergone US Army officer training at Fort Benning, Georgia. He had been imprisoned in 1958 for taking part in an attempt to overthrow Batista but was released with the triumph of the revolution, returning to the Army until he was imprisoned again for helping former Batista Army officers to leave the country. He was finally exiled to the US.

San Román's second in command was Erneido Oliva González, another former Cuban Army officer trained in Panama, who left Cuba in 1960 when he was forced to leave the Army.

Guatemala

As the intention was not to train any forces in the United States, because of the risks of discovery that the US government was backing the operation, it was decided to move the training of the exile force to Guatemala, where President Miguel Ydígoras Fuentes had just broken relations with Cuba. The Guatemalan president offered first to create training camps in the Petén area, to the north of the country, which was almost unpopulated and far from the main cities. Ydígoras asked Roberto Alejos, a local entrepreneur and close associate of his (known as John Black to the CIA), to negotiate with the CIA; during meetings held on 30 and 31 May 1960, he offered to house a training camp in his country, offering the Finca La Helvetia coffee plantation belonging to Alejos in Retalhuleu Department (near the Pacific coast), called Base JTrax. The barracks and training fields were built in late July. In the meantime, on 8 July, the CIA asked Alejos to check if the runway at the town of Retalhuleu could be used as an air base. They also inspected the runways at Puerto San José, on the Pacific coast, and Flores at Petén.

As the runway at Retalhuleu was not in good condition to operate planes such as the DC-4, Alejos contracted the Thompson Cornwall

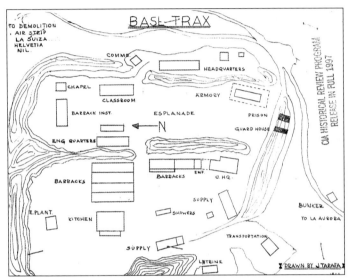

Diagram of the barracks at Finca La Helvetia.

Corporation to build a runway measuring 1,500 x 35 metres, a control tower, barracks and other buildings, with construction starting on 3 August and finishing on 13 September in the presence of Ydígoras, while all buildings were completed by 30 September. The new base was called Base JMadd by the CIA and Base Rayo by the Cubans. The air operation was covert, as if it was a Guatemalan Air Force Base, and the planes used for training were painted in their colours. Ydígoras explained that they were planes purchased from the United States as part of the Military Assistance Plan. Colonel Manuel Villafaña was later named as the head of the Fuerza Aérea de Liberación (FAL).

A cover was also required for the training of ground forces, so the Guatemalan Army organized a Paratroop Platoon, under the command of Lieutenant Benedicto Lucas, with 30 men, who were installed in barracks at the entrance of La Helvetia, called Finca La Viña. Officially, they were the only troops training in the area and they were sent to train in anti-guerrilla operations. Alejos declared to the press that there were troops being trained on his farm to be prepared against possible aggression from Cuba, but that there were no Cubans there.[1] La Helvetia also had a small runway, unpaved and 490 metres long, used by small planes.

Despite the Guatemalan government offering the participation of Guatemalan troops in the invasion, this was rejected by the CIA.[2]

---

1 *Prensa Libre* newspaper, Guatemala, 11 January 1961.
2 *Contrapoder* magazine, Los Cubanos y la CIA en Guatemala, Rodrigo Fernández Ordóñez, Guatemala, April 2015.

Two CIA instructors with a member of Brigade 2506.

Troops of Brigade 2506 at La Helvetia during training.

Assault Brigade 2506

From July to November, the recruits were trained in guerrilla operations, while the force started to grow in numbers, with more and more men being enlisted, mainly in Miami, reaching 160 in September and about 300 by October.

In September, while undergoing training, one of the recruits of the brigade, Carlos Rafael Santana, known as "Carlay", died in an accident. To honour him, his comrades decided to name the Assault Brigade with his serial number: 2506.

In the meantime, in mid-August, Eisenhower had approved a $13 million budget and the use of Defense Department personnel and equipment, but specifically ruled out US soldiers in a combat role.

They were originally organized into the Grey and Black teams, the first comprising up to eight men and the other of 20 to 25. The first had an intelligence officer, psychological warfare officer, armaments officer, demolition officer, radio operator and commanding officer.[3] The Grey teams would infiltrate first and train local forces to expand the guerrillas and prepare the terrain for the Black teams.

A 13 August 1960 CIA memorandum gives some idea of the original plan:

In the discussion of air suppression operations which were scheduled to begin in November 1960, the destruction of the Castro Air Force on D-Day was to be achieved by attacks on eight principal airfields; and, in addition, D-Day air strikes also were scheduled for non-military bases with the intent to cripple the mobile reserves in the barracks and to destroy materiel.

The report also detailed the use of air cover with fighters: "Provision for fighter escort for air assault forces, air cover of amphibious force, and on-call close air support of ground operational force in all surface operations encompassing approximately 100 square miles of area.

Estimated aircraft requirement two fighters on station during daylight hours."

The plan consisted of nine small air-maritime infiltrations between August and 15 November 1960, while on D-Day the initial attack was to be a 170-man combat assault force airlifted into Cuba, carrying crew-served weapons, mortars, recoilless rifles, small arms, bazookas and demolitions. To back up the initial strike force, there was to be another 170-man contingency force which was "subsequent to delivery of [the] strike force on an on-call basis, for execution within 6 hours of return from [the] first airlift".[4]

As the plan stated a limit of a 450-mile radius for air operations, this meant they had to be made from the Yucatan Peninsula, the continental United States, the Bahamas, the Cayman Islands or Montego Bay in Jamaica, the last being at the extreme range for attacks on La Habana.

In the meantime, photo reconnaissance was considered necessary before the end of September, especially to determine the capabilities and deployment of the FAR, as it was considered the main threat to the brigade's activities once landed. Lockheed U-2 and RF-101 Voodoo planes were used to make a photo survey of the main bases, and also over the possible areas of ground operations, but as the pictures were taken more than six months before the actual landing, some of the information they contained was out of date by then. For example, the photos showed that the runway at Playa Girón was not finished yet,

---

3 *The Inevitable Battle*, Juan Carlos Rodríguez, Editorial Capitán San José, La Habana 2009.

4 *Official history of the Bay of Pigs Operation*, Jack Pfeiffer, Central Intelligence Agency, 1979.

Paratroopers training at Finca La Suiza, about 4km from La Helvetia.

A formation during training at La Helvetia.

Troops of the brigade, with the definitive uniform and flag of the unit, during training at La Helvetia.

Training with a recoilless gun. The unpaved runway of La Helvetia was used as a firing range, with targets at the end of the runway.

so machinery to make the runway operational were sent with the first landing waves, using space that could better be used for supplies for the ground troops. When the brigade landed, they noticed the runway was actually ready for use. They also determined that the FAR was using several airports as bases, when in fact they had San Antonio de los Baños as their sole air base, and also sometimes deployed to Santiago de Cuba. This led to the bombing on 15 April of Ciudad Libertad aerodrome, containing the command of the force but no operational combat airplanes.

The original plan also analyzed the possibilities of a Cuban air strike against the air bases used by the exiles if they departed from Florida or the Bahamas, as they could be in range for the Douglas B-26s, Hawker Sea Furies and Lockheed T-33s, but it was considered that the FAR did not have enough power to cause severe damage as only a few planes could be used for such a mission.

The August 1960 USAF report after the U-2 flights identified the various types and numbers of aircraft, including an estimate that among others there were some 30-odd combat types, including Douglas B-26s, Sea Furies and Lockheed T-33s. Of these, USAF intelligence estimated that there were 12 B-26s, six to eight Sea Furies and four T-33s, which might be used for reconnaissance or light bombing missions. The truth is that this report was very optimistic, as most of those planes were not operational.

On 4 November, the information arrived at Base Trax that training must change from guerrilla operations to a conventional amphibious assault, as the CIA had changed its mind on how activities to overthrow Castro must be organized. The first plan was to land in Trinidad, a small town located between the southern coast of Cuba and the Escambray mountains, where there was a small runway

and a harbour, that could be used to support the rebels. In case the operation went wrong, they could move to the mountains and join the anti-Castro guerrillas.

Only 83 Cubans kept training on guerrilla operations and were sent on 5 December to a farm near Puerto San José, Escuintla Department, on the Pacific coast, near to an airfield that was built for training of paratroopers. This place was called "Garrapatenango" by the Cubans due to the abundance of "garrapatas" (ticks). After two weeks they were sent to Fort Clayton in the Panama Canal Zone. Only 47 were selected to continue the training and were sent to Louisiana, finishing by mid-January 1961, when they were sent back to Retalhuleu. These teams, called Inca, were later sent back to Miami, and from there infiltrated to support the guerrillas and underground groups operating against Castro.

The new plan also stated that the entire brigade would be landed at the same place, instead of making small insertions in different places to support the various guerrilla groups operating in the country. This was developed because of the huge quantity of military equipment being received by Castro from the Soviet Bloc, including artillery and tanks, which in a short time would pose a big threat to any counter-revolutionary action. The guerrilla plan supposed a long-term fight until defeating Castro, and this rearming process, together with the organization of the Revolutionary Militias, would make things very difficult. Faster action was therefore required, supposing that, with a portion of Cuban soil liberated from Castro's domination, the anti-Castro organizations operating underground in Cuba would increase their operations and people would join the rebel forces, leading

Two C-46s and a C-54 at Retalhuleu Air Base. The small white building to the left was the base command post.

B-26s delivered to the Brigade, wearing Guatemalan Air Force markings, seen at Retalhuleu.

One of the B-26s used for spares, lying to one side of Retalhuleu Air Base.

A view of Retalhuleu Air Base during training, seen from the control tower looking north. Two operational B-26s and two written-off and used for spares can be seen, as well as two C-54s. To the left is the barracks used by the Guatemalan soldiers who provided security for the base.

A B-26 performing a bombing practice near Retalhuleu. The bomb bay is open.

to a swift victory. With the new plan, the 300-man force had to be expanded to 1,500 in order to undertake the planned landing.

There were two main problems in increasing the force. The first problem was to find enough exiled Cubans wanting to enlist, caused by the differences of the leaders of the FRD, who wanted to have only their followers as recruits and would not accept the followers of other leaders. Also, none wanted former Batista Army veterans. This was solved by the end of 1960 and recruits started to arrived in Guatemala more quickly, reaching 500 by January. The other issue was that Base

Trax was built for only 200 men and was already having trouble with the 300 men that were there in November. During the rainy season, it was almost impossible to reach and supplies had to be taken by tractors. The farm was in the middle of the hills, with an unpaved road from Retalhuleu which became very difficult to travel.

After he won the elections for US president, John F. Kennedy was briefed on the plan on 27 November. Although he was concerned about the small size of the brigade, he decided to go ahead with the plan.

The barracks used by the officers of the Fuerza Aérea de Liberación, seen today.

One of the tiny buildings of the original base command, currently used by the Guatemalan Air Force.

A B-26, with Guatemalan Air Force markings, could be seen at Retalhuleu on 16 January 1961, when journalists visited the base, with the intention of making people believe there were no Cubans there.

Ground forces

As the ground forces of Brigade 2506 were growing, in the first days of 1961 they were finally organized into seven battalions, reaching a total of 1,511 infantrymen, with another 300 men in the support force. Only 135 of them were former soldiers, whereas the biggest group were students - 240 of them. The rest were a hodgepodge of doctors, lawyers, businessmen, peasants and fishermen, some as young as 16 and one as old as 61.[5]

They were organized following US Army methods, but despite being labelled battalions, they only had the strength of a company, with about 180 men each. The order of battle consisted on the 1st Paratrooper Battalion (with 177 men), the 2nd, 5th and 6th Infantry Battalions (with 175 men), the 3rd Armored Battalion (with 175 men), the 4th Heavy Weapons Battalion (with 114 men) and the 7th Infantry Battalion (with 175 men), the latter of which was a reserve which remained in Guatemala and wasn't deployed. There was also a diver platoon with six Special Demolition Teams of four men, three teams armed with sub-machine guns and three teams with Browning M1918A2 machine guns, totaling 68 men. To assist the men wounded in battle, there was a surgical team of 18 men.

The support force comprised the headquarters and service company (156 men), with two squadrons armed with sub-machine guns and two equipped with twelve 2½-ton REO M-35 trucks armed with 12.7 Browning M2 machine guns. The vehicles also included eleven ¼-ton Jeeps, nine ¼-ton tractors, an aviation fuel tanker truck with 3,000

5   *The Bay of Pigs*, Howard Jones, Oxford University Press, New York, 2008.

gallons of fuel, a tractor crane, one bulldozer, four 400 gallon water trailers and 13 trailers.

There was a Tank Platoon of 24 men trained secretly at Fort Knox and equipped with five M-41 Walker Bulldog medium tanks, but they and the trucks were delivered from the USS *San Marcos* while at sea prior to the invasion. The small tank force was planned to act in support of the infantry and not as an ordinary armoured unit, with the few tanks dispersed all along the landing area.

The infantry units received twenty-two 60mm mortars, twenty 81mm mortars, seven 107mm M-30s, eighteen 57mm M-18A-1 recoilless guns and four 75mm M-20s, 47 M-20 "Super Bazooka" rocket launchers, nine M-2 flame throwers and 49 Browning 7.62mm machine guns (M-1919A6) and 108 of 12.7mm (M-2HB). There was also a total of 3,000 light weapons, which included M-1 Garand and Johnson M-1941 rifles and M-1A1 carbines for the infantry, Springfield M1903A4s for the snipers, M3A1 sub-machine guns for the paratroopers, M1A1 and M1928A1 Thompsons for the headquarters and the Special Demolition Teams and Browning M1918A2 machine guns for the support of the infantry. All soldiers used Browning M1911A-1 .45 pistols and grenades of different types. Each soldier also landed with 160 rounds for their rifles.

Each battalion was organized into companies, comprising platoons and smaller squads. Each squad was of nine men, two of them with Browning Automatic Rifles (BAR), and each company had a squad with two 7.62mm machine guns. The E Company of each battalion carried two bazookas, two 7.62mm machine guns, a 57mm recoilless gun, and an 81mm and 60mm mortar.

The Fuerza Aérea de Liberación

To provide some air power for the operation, 12 former US Navy AD-5 Skyraiders were considered, but as the model was not used in Latin America, were discarded as they could not meet the non-attributability (to the US) requirement.

On 21 July, the CIA decided to use the B-26 Invader, and a tiny air force was organized from August at Base Rayo, starting training in September with six B-26s delivered to the Fuerza Aérea Guatemalteca, which were borrowed from them to use on the initial training of the crews. One of them, FAG 420, made a belly landing at Retalhuleu on an unknown date during the brigade pilots' training. For some time they were joined by two TB-26s, with dual controls for training, from the District of Columbia Air National Guard (ANG) at Eglin AFB, before the definitive planes were delivered. Major Billy B. Campbell, who was initially put in charge of the B-26 air training programme in Guatemala, said: "These aircraft were much lighter and much faster

The control tower at Retalhuleu. The building retains most of its original shape, as built in 1960.

The original supply depots of Retalhuleu Air Base, built in 1960, which are currently used as small hangars by the Guatemalan Air Force.

than the airplanes we finally received."[6]

Pilots from the Alabama ANG went to Base Rayo to train the Cuban pilots, who were selected from among those exiles with some flying experience; however, some of them only had about 100 flying hours, and almost none of them on twin-engined planes. The training plan provided 20 hours of ground school and a total of 20 sorties, with 51 hours of flying time during a minimum of 15 days from the first flight.

By 23 September, Cuban personnel at Base Rayo numbered 39 pilots (for both the B-26 and transport planes), two navigators, 18 mechanics, a chaplain and a doctor.

The Invader was selected because they were easy to get from surplus stocks, were easy and cheap to use and had the range to operate from Guatemala or Nicaragua while supporting the guerrilla operations. Also, the model was in use by the FAR in Cuba, despite them using the B-26C version with plexiglas nose for a bomber and the Brigade receiving B-26Bs with eight 12.7mm machine guns on a closed nose. The B-26s would have no air cover from fighters during the operations, but the original plan was that they would operate alone on small air strike missions where the FAR would not have the assets to intercept them on time, as they did not have any early warning system, which was proved during the flights between 1959 and 1960 supporting anti-revolution activities.

The B-26s were requested by the CIA, "with eight .50 caliber

machine guns in the nose, rocket-launching system (for four rockets on each wing), pylon fuel tanks under each wing, and bomb bays capable of accepting either 250 or 500lb bombs. Four such aircraft are required by 1 September 1960, the remaining six will be required by 15 October 1960."[7] But, the CIA added, "of more significance, however, was the plan to add to the plane's firepower by adding three internal guns to both the left and the right wings - bringing the total of .50 caliber forward-firing machine guns to either 14 or 12". However, this modification was not made because there wasn't enough time and budget. The Defense Department's initial estimate of the cost of the B-26 aircraft was approximately $11,000 for those which were flyable, and $27,500 for planes which would have to be taken out of storage.

The Air Force notified the CIA that four B-26s configured "in accordance with your requirement" would be available from Kelly AFB on 30 August 1960, and would be dropped out of the USAF aircraft inventory and made available to the Agency on an interdepartmental transfer. All the B-26s would receive Guatemalan Air Force serials and colours while in use at Base Rayo, changing them for FAR colours and serials for the combat operations. They were different from the real Guatemalan planes as the latter did not use drop tanks and the disposition of the machine guns on the nose was different.

During training, on 14 and 15 November, William Beale and Connie Seigrist, two of the CIA pilots training the Cubans, flew B-26s out of Base Rayo on strafing missions against an insurrection of the Guatemalan Armed Forces that had started in the towns of Zacapa and Puerto Barrios. The towns were on the Caribbean coast and the Guatemalan government feared the rebels would expect support from Cuba, so they asked the CIA to get support from the Cubans, who were put on maximum alert. The US Navy deployed two Lockheed P-2V Neptunes to patrol the seas between Cuba and Guatemala and also sent a destroyer.

Connie Seigrist recalls:

Col. Batres flew down from Guatemala City on this particular afternoon to Retalhuleu for our air and ground assistance to help quell the insurrection. It came to light in his request for our assistance the Guatemala Air Force pilots under his command refused to take military action against their own countrymen and we were his last resort to help in saving the Ydigoras Government. Late at night we received permission from our Field Commander to assist Col. Batres. We immediately prepared three C-46s and Cuban ground troops to be flown to Puerto Barrios escorted by two B-26s in the early morning to arrive at daybreak. I flew one of the B-26s. Col. Batres' instructions were for our B-26s to soften the airfield with our firepower to enable the C-46s to land with the Cuban ground troops without danger from retaliatory ground fire. The Cuban ground troops were then to take over and secure the airfield. Also in our instructions we were not to shoot into any operations or residential buildings on the airfield because Col. Batres' intelligence source reported the local politicians unsympathetic to the revolt were being held hostage in the airport buildings and we should take all precaution not to harm them. We arrived in our B-26s as planned and proceeded to strafe and rocket gun emplacements, open sheds, revetments, thick bushes, or any place that could camouflage ground firing troops. By the time the C-46s arrived I was well convinced we had nullified any possible return action from the ground. Neither of our B-26s was hit by ground fire. ... The three C-46s returned to Retalhuleu and we in our B-26s landed at Guatemala City per Col. Batres' previous instructions. We remained for the day on the City

---

6 *Official history of the Bay of Pigs Operation*, Jack Pfeiffer, Central Intelligence Agency, 1979.

7 *Official history of the Bay of Pigs Operation*, Jack Pfeiffer, Central Intelligence Agency, 1979.

airfield to fly cover for some Guatemala Air Force C-47s landing troops on a mountain airfield located halfway to Puerto Barrios. … I flew alone. The C-47s made their landing just before dark. They met no resistance and I returned to Retalhuleu as instructed by Col. Batres. Col. Batres instructed me the next morning to patrol the entire south coastal area from the mountains to the ocean and from the Mexico border to the El Salvador border. My instructions were to strafe anything moving on the highway or into any grouping of people. I patrolled the entire day and sighted nothing. After landing back in Retalhuleu I learned Col. Batres had flown to Puerto Barrios to negotiate with the leaders of the revolt and the revolt was over.[8]

In total, 218 Cubans were deployed on the C-46s and only one of them landed. The Cubans fired from the door and emergency windows, while the pilot thought it was an ambuscade and took off immediately, returning to Retalhuleu.[9] In the meantime, two C-124 Globemaster planes were sent from the US to Retalhuleu with supplies and weapons for the operations against the rebels.

The four B-26Bs delivered by the USAF at Kelly AFB in August were joined in December by six more planes. They were followed by a request for six to eight extra planes, but two of them were used for spares at Retalhuleu and not used on further operations. They included serials 44-34315, 44-34590, 44,35242, 44-35420, 44-35574, 44-35782, 44-35698, 44-35789, 44-35821, 44-35830, 44-35839, 44-35845 and 44-35896, recorded as delivered by the USAF at Davis-Monthan AFB to Intermountain Aviation on behalf of the recorded end-user, Caribbean Marine Aero Corp.

The squadron was organized under the command of Joaquín "Pupy" Varela, and training began firing at rafts made of empty fuel tanks dropped on Atitlán Lake to the north-west of Base Rayo.

Five pilots were considered ready by the end of the year, with six more still in training. Consideration was given to using US contract pilots in case it was necessary. In the end, 17 Cubans were trained as B-26 pilots: Joaquín Varela y Vieytes, Mario Álvarez Cortina, Miguel Carro Suárez, Luis Cosme Toribio, José Crespo Grasso, Matías Farías Riesgo, Daniel Fernández Mon, Crispin García, René Garcia, Alfredo González Caballero, Gonzalo Herrera, Osvaldo Piedra Neguerela, Gustavo Ponzoa, Ignacio Rojas, Antonio Soto, Raúl Vianello Alacán and Mario Zuñiga Rivas.

The following were trained as navigators: Manuel Villafaña Martínez, Esteban Bovo Carás, Oscar Vega, Lorenzo Pérez Lorenzo, Gastón Pérez, José Fernández, Nildo Batista Fernández, Luis Ardois, Alfredo Maza Barrios, Rafael García Pujol, Ángel López, Eduardo Barea Guinea, Tomás Afont, Salvador Miralles, Eduardo González, González Romero, Demetrio Pérez, Benito González, Gustavo Villoldo and Alberto Pérez Sordo.

Besides the CIA personnel and other US civilians contracted (which totalled around 50 men), nine men from Washington DC ANG (which was retiring its B-26s), 33 from Alabama ANG (which was still using the B-26 and making the transition to the F-84), 21 from Arkansas ANG, 14 from Georgia ANG and two from California ANG acted as instructors for the pilots and ground crew, as well as on the logistical flights from the US to Guatemala, with a total of 150 men being involved.

The B-26s also flew some pre-invasion overflights of Cuba out of Retalhulcu, about one per week from October to late December, flights that lasted up to 8½ hours and were undertaken in order to

8   *Memoirs*, Connie Seigrist, University of Texas Dallas, William M. Leary Papers, Box 11 Folder 9.
9   *Contrapoder* magazine, Los Cubanos y la CIA en Guatemala, Rodrigo Fernández Ordóñez, Guatemala, April 2015.

Barracks used by the Guatemalan forces that provided security for the base during the training of the Cubans.

Four C-46s and a C-54 at Puerto Cabezas.

drop leaflets and test the Cuban defences, while US listening stations in Florida and elsewhere noted all Cuban reactions.

In November, once the Cubans had met certain tests that had been given to them, a number of the pilots who were discontent asked to be transferred back to Miami. Among this dozen were the second-in-command of the Air Force (Leslie Nobregas), the Chief of the C-54 squadron (Orlando Alvarez Builla) and the Chief of the C-46 squadron (Juan Perez), so Eduardo Ferrer became the head of this last squadron.

Transports

For transport duties, four Curtiss C-46s were purchased by the CIA's airline, Air America, from Air Asia for $75,000 each - serials B-850 (c/n22451), B-864 (c/n22362), B-866 (c/n22366) and B-870 (c/n22252). They were delivered to a Cuban company acting as a façade, Los Hermanos Sebastián y Gómez, owned by Manuel F. Goudie, and, in turn leased to the Cuban exile organization, the FRD. The B-850 and B-864 left Tainan, Taiwan, on 3 September 1960 and arrived at Oakland, California, three days later, while the B-866 left on 18 September and arrived on the 21st. The B-870 left on 24 September and flew directly to San Antonio, Texas, arriving on 30 September. The four planes were then handed over to the Cubans and flown to San José Airfield on the Pacific coast of Guatemala, and then to Base Rayo. The planes were delivered together with some C-54s directly from USAF stocks, and together with the first four B-26s formed the first units of the tiny rebel air force. The transport pilots were trained by Air America pilots Connie Seigrist and William Beale, later joined by Douglas R. Price, first at San José and later at Base Rayo. The Cuban C-46 squadron was put under the command of an unknown Cuban, later replaced by Eduardo B. Ferrer when the former decided to return to Miami. To get C-46 pilots combat-ready required only five sorties with a total flight time of 21 hours over a minimum time of seven days; it was provided that the training requirements could be satisfied during the course of local cargo runs between Base Rayo and the San José airfield.

By March 1961, the C-46 serialled 866 had been destroyed in a crash and subsequent fire. A replacement was offered with the plane serial N9894Z (c/n 32942, ex 44-77546), on 4 April 1961, but it is not known if this arrived in time for the operations. Another four planes - c/nos 32992 (N9935Z, ex 44-77596), 33451 (N9895Z ex B-918 and ex 44-78055), 22343 (N9459Z ex 44-78520) and 33445 (N91293, ex 44-78049) - were delivered to Los Hermanos Sebastián y Gómez, but their purchase was only registered after the operations, so it is not known if all of them were used at Bay of Pigs or to support subsequent actions to help the anti-Castro guerrillas.

All were later officially registered in Panama, with known registrations being HP-314 (former B-866), HP-314P (former N9895Z), HP-316 (former B-850), HP-322P (former N9459Z) and probably also HP-315 (former N91293 and 44-78049). No Panamanian registrations are known for the C-46s B-864 and B-870.

Since they started to operate from Guatemala, the C-46s themselves received three-digit serials that were more or less arbitrary, intended to make them look like Fuerza Aérea Guatemalteca aircraft: B-850 is known to have become 857, and B-864 simply became 864. On 6 November 1960, C-46 292 was used for a flight to the Escambray mountains. Other C-46 serials known from the actual invasion are 877, 875, 788 and 855. It is believed that 1887, or at least 887, was the former C-46 N9895Z (ex 44-78055).[10]

Along with the C-46s were the Douglas C-54Gs, which would be initially used to carry recruited men, stores and various kinds of cargo between the United States and Retalhuleu. The first two were delivered to the former Opa Locka Naval Air Station (unused by the US Navy since 1959) from Eglin Air Force Base. From Opa Locka, they flew at night to Guatemala. Some flights were also performed directly from Eglin and other bases. The C-54 squadron was placed under the command of Orlando Alvarez Builla.

They performed air drop missions to help the guerrillas in the Escambray mountains. The first took place on 28 September 1960, but the operation was not a success, as the supplies landed seven miles from the reception area, falling into the hands of Castro's militia instead of the rebels. The plane, probably former US serial 45-558, was lost when returning to Retalhuleu; it had engine problems and had to make an emergency landing at Comitán in Mexico, where it was confiscated, despite the crew being released.

In October, another C-54, this time a D model, was delivered to replace it through Los Hermanos Sebastián y Gomez. The former USAF serial 42-72523 and Panamanian serial HP-321P was the sole example of this version with the Brigade.

The other C-54G, serialled 45-592, was lost in October, when, returning from an air drop training flight, the plane touched a tree with a wingtip over Guatemala and the pilot, Ed Smith, crash landed on Champerico beach close to Retalhuleu.

This second plane lost was replaced by another C-54G bought through Los Hermanos Sebastián y Gomez, with serial HP-320P (c/n 36063, ex 45-610 and N4000A).

They were followed by another four (45-565, 45-520, 45-631,

and 45-636) that belonged to the 1045th Operational Evaluation & Training Group (which in fact was the DPD or Development Projects Division, the CIA's air arm), assigned to the unit between 7-10 November 1960 and remaining with them until June or July 1961. Between 20-22 February 1961, another four C-54Gs were delivered to the unit (45-550, 45-561, 45-579 and 45-611) and remained with them until June or July 1961, making a fleet of 10 C-54s with the Brigade at the time of the invasion. Despite sometimes being flown by Cuban or US pilots, in most cases they were Czech or Polish, contracted by the CIA for operations crossing the Iron Curtain.

The C-54D received the fake serial 6600, and the others 6604, 6605, 6606, 6609, 7001, 7003, 7701 and 7702.

In the meantime, supply drops to guerrillas in the Escambray hills were resumed on 6 November 1960, using the C-46 with serial 292, and between then and March 1961, 66 additional drops were flown from Retalhuleu. These flights took between 11-14 hours from departure to return, depending on the type of aircraft used and the actual destination, with an overall flying distance of 1,600-1,800 nautical miles.[11]

According to a CIA document: "In all, about 151,000lb of arms, ammunition and equipment were transported by air. Not more than 69,000lb of this was actually dropped; the rest was returned to base. Of this 69,000lb, at least 46,000lb were captured by Castro forces, who recovered all or a large part of ten drops, compared with our agents, who recovered three."[12] The problem was that there was no direct communication between the guerrillas and Base Rayo. The same CIA document also says:

There were four such successes in all, out of 30 missions flown up to 21 April 1961. ... The first of these took place on 30 December after numerous attempts beginning in mid-October. There were 13 unsuccessful attempts during January and February. The third success took place on 3 March, when three agents were dropped (previous attempts to drop them had been made on 7 February and 27 February). The fourth successful drop was on 29 March.

Since the beginning of 1961, when Cuba started to receive 37mm guns from the Soviet Union, but especially after Castro's forces performed operations against the guerrillas in the Escambray mountains, all the drop missions in the area received heavy fire from the Revolutionary Militias. On 5 March 1961, a C-54 was forced to land at Montego Bay, Jamaica, when returning from a mission over Cuba, where one of its engines had been hit by ground fire. Four days later, the crew was picked up at Kingston airport by another C-54 arriving at night. The damaged C-54 was recovered shortly after.

In the meantime, when the plan was changed for a conventional assault, which included the dropping of paratroopers, training for them was required and a special battalion was created in November 1960. These troops performed training at Suiza farm, called Base Halcón by the Cubans, near La Helvetia (Base Trax), which also belonged to Alejos. In December, they moved to "Garrapatenango", close to San José airfield, from where planes took them to practice jumps. In February 1961 they performed two drops over the nearby San Juan farm.

The Brigade also received a single Beech AT-11 and two Helio Couriers, one of them serialled HP-322P (c/n 525), re-serialled TG-DOF around March 1961, for liaison duties. There was also an

10 'Air America at the Bay of Pigs', article by Dr Joe F. Leeker, University of Texas, 4 March 2013.

11 'Air America at the Bay of Pigs', article by Dr Joe F. Leeker, University of Texas, 4 March 2013.

12 Inspector General's Survey of the Cuban Operation, Central Intelligence Agency, October 1961.

The Catalina named "Swan", some B-26s and a C-46 at Puerto Cabezas.

One of the B-26s at Puerto Cabezas, after receiving the serial FAR-933. This is probably the plane that went to Florida to act as if defecting from Cuba.

American-manned Consolidated PBY-5A Catalina serialled HP-289 (c/n 22022), officially owned by Turismo Aéreo SA of Panama, and flown directly from Puerto Cabezas with fake serial 289. It had been fitted with electronic equipment at Miami in early 1961 and was named "Swan Island" (to confuse the Cubans with radio broadcasts from Swan Island in Honduras). Its mission was to fly at altitude around the invasion area in Cuba and to retransmit radio broadcasts back to CIA Headquarters at Langley, Virginia. The American crew of this PBY consisted of Air America pilot Don Teeters, Philip Gibbony, Philip Ingoglia, John S. Lewis, Joel F. Kilgore, Harry P. Rahm and Joe M. Skipper.[13]

Finally, a Lockheed L-1649 Constellation was acquired for the Brigade and used on 29 January 1961 to take 50 reporters to Base Rayo and Trax, following a report in the *New York Times* by journalist Paul Kennedy, stating that an invasion force was being assembled in Guatemala to act against Castro. All the Brigade forces were removed from the base and replaced by a Guatemalan paratrooper platoon, to show the press that there was nothing there except a Guatemalan Air Force and Army base. It was also planned to be used as an evacuation area for personnel at Base Rayo.

Nicaragua

Base Rayo was considered too far from central Cuba, about 1,400km, to conduct operations on the island, so another option has to be found. Mexico and the Bahamas were considered but discarded. Puerto Barrios, in Guatemala, was also considered as a refuelling point for B-26s returning from operations over Cuba, and a plan was even developed for an air strike of six planes against an unknown target in Cuba to take place on 26 November from there, with the planes being loaded with bombs at Base Rayo before going to the other airport to refuel. This mission was ultimately changed to an air drop of supplies, with only one plane, and took place on 5 December, but the pilot could not find the air drop zone and returned to Puerto Barrios.

Then, in October 1960, Nicaraguan president Luis Somoza agreed to concede the use of the airfield and harbour at Puerto Cabezas, on the Caribbean coast of his country, just 950km from Bay of Pigs, both for aerial operations and to embark the landing force. The new base was code-named JMTide and called Happy Valley by the CIA crews.

Somoza also offered the use of his North American P-51D Mustang fighters, but they lacked the range to escort the B-26s to and from Cuba and protect the planes over the combat zone. The CIA also studied the possible use by the Brigade of P-51s or Vought F4U Corsairs, but again, the problem was the long distance from Puerto Cabezas, which

gave them only a few minutes over the area of operations to protect the bombers.

In March 1961, one of the Helio Couriers flying to President Ydigoras' farm had an accident while landing and was destroyed, although the occupants escaped safely (the other Helio continued operating for Air America from 1962 in Asia). The C-46 with former serial B-866 was sent to recover the remains of the plane, but on the approach they hit a tree with a wing and crashed, with the two pilots and nine passengers (which were going to disassemble the Courier) escaping unhurt but a man on the ground being killed.

Shortly before the invasion, on 28 March 1961, training flights and those over Cuba were suspended, as the planes were needed to move the Brigade troops from Ratalhuleu to Puerto Cabezas. Another C-46 remained out of action with Connie Seigrist at the controls. He recalled:

> We needed an auxiliary field in preparation for the invasion. … I searched out an area of fairly level open grass land nearby that appeared it could support the weight of C-46s and B-26s. I landed the fourth C-46 there and immediately it sank down into the ground. That C-46 was rendered unavailable for the invasion because of the time involved for digging it out. I flew it to Miami after the invasion.

This left only five C-46s and 10 C-54s available for the invasion, which moved its base from Base Rayo to Happy Valley from 2 April.

By 2 April, a gunnery, bomb and rocket range had been located some 45 miles north-east of Puerto Cabezas in the vicinity of the Cayos Miskitos Islands. In a three-hour period on 3 April, 11 aircraft had arrived at Happy Valley - six B-26s, three C-46s and two C-54s - with the transport aircraft scheduled to return to Base Rayo for additional cargo and passengers. These aircraft brought in 169 Cuban personnel. On the same day, two of the B-26s were sent to inspect the bomb and gunnery range, with Captain Quintana of the Nicaraguan Gardia Nacional riding in one of the B-26s as an observer. On 4 and 5 April, 17 sorties were planned for the first pilots of the B-26s. The ordnance load for these sorties was to be two 500lb bombs, four 200lb fragmentation bombs, four rockets and 800 rounds of .50 calibre ammunition.

In the meantime, the C-54s also moved the ground troops in the first days of April, and one of them was used to carry the small boats with outboard engines that would be used in the landing. The main

13 'Air America at the Bay of Pigs', article by Dr Joe F. Leeker, University of Texas, 4 March 2013.

operation to move the Brigade to Puerto Cabezas took place during 10 and 11 April, using all the C-54s and C-46s available. A total of 1,300 troops were moved to Puerto Cabezas, leaving only the 160 airborne troops which would be flown directly from Base Rayo to the drop zones in Cuba on D-Day.

Once in Puerto Cabezas, the B-26s had to be painted in FAR colours, and paint was urgently requested urgently at Eglin AFB to be flown to Nicaragua. The plan was to paint them with a 3ft blue stripe on the wing to differentiate them from the FAR planes, and with fake serials, which in many cases were repeated. For example, there were two planes with serial 931, two with 933 and three with 935. As well as these serials, there were the following: 915, 923, 927, 928, 929, 930, 945, 950, 955, 960, 965 and 985, totalling at least 19 different serials. As records differ between 16 and 18 planes used, it is probable that serials were changed during the operations.

More B-26s

Further B-26s with former serials 44-35242, 44-34376, 44-34620 and 44-34682 were registered by Los Hermanos Sebastián y Gómez in Panama as, respectively, HP-318 (later as HP-322), HP-323, HP-318P and HP-319, and delivered to the Brigade. The planes were modified with long-range ferry tanks installed in the bomb bays, but the modification took its time and they arrived late, being delivered to Happy Valley. General Lyman Lemnitzer, Chairman of the Joint Chiefs of Staff stated that:

> The afternoon or night of D-Day 4 B-26s were made available which we had been preparing for the Laos operations. Then 4 more were made available on D+1. In addition to that, we offered 5 T-33s and CIA accepted 4. On D+1 action was initiated to use C-130s in dropping ammunition on the beachhead. The aircraft were moved to Kelly, the packing crews were on their way, and the crews were set up for the drops on the night of D+1 but they never went into action.[14]

Connie Seigrist had some particular objections to the modifications, saying: "These replacement B-26s had ferry tanks strapped permanently in the bomb bays. In my estimation, they were flying bombs - we never used them. Like the T-33s, it was too late anyway to have used them."[15] He also says the planes had a total of 10 machine guns, so most probably they had six on the nose and four under the wings.

As Seigrist states, the four B-26s were delivered together with four unidentified T-33s, which were prepared at Eglin AFB with Louisiana National Air Guard pilots to be used to provide fighter cover, but the order for them to fly was never given. The same happened with a few C-130s that were prepared to deliver ammunition to the beachhead during the night, but the go-ahead order also never came.

Naval Forces

A small transport force was organized to carry the troops from Puerto Cabezas to the landing zone, using ships chartered to a company called García Steamship Lines, which belonged to a Cuban family. The ships were the *Houston*, *Atlantico*, *Caribe* and *Rio Escondido*.

Five ships of the N3 Coastal Cargo Ships type, built during the Second World War, were purchased. N3-S-A1 types the *Houston* and *Lake Charles* displaced 1,791 tons, while the N3-S-A2s *Atlántico* and

14 'Foreign Relations of the United States, 1961-1963, Volume X, Cuba, 1961-1962. 121'. Memorandum of Conversation, Washington, 18 April 1961.

15 *Memoirs*, Connie Seigrist, University of Texas Dallas, William M. Leary Papers, Box 11 Folder 9.

Caribe displaced 1,896 tons. The *Río Escondido*'s, sub-type and origin is unknown.

The *Lake Charles* was originally built as the *William Bursley* in 1942, had hit a mine in 1948 in the North Sea and suffered a collision in 1954. The ship had the names *Damara* and *Pietro Canale* before being named *Lake Charles*. She was finally lost in Grand Cayman in 1964. She was prepared to be used as a hospital ship and received the code name "Atún" (Tuna). The *Houston* was built as the *Freeman Hatch* and later became the *Charles M*.

Built as the *John Leckie*, the *Caribe* received its new name in 1948. After the invasion, in 1961, it became the *Pensacola* and served until 1966. The *Atlántico* was built as the *Judah P. Baker* but in 1944 became a Polish vessel with the name *Kutno*, until in 1947 returning to the US Marine Corps and one year later becoming the *Atlántico*. She was scrapped in 1963. During the operation she used the code name "Tiburón" (Shark).

Another ship of the type, named *Santa Ana*, was used to carry a special unit with the intention to land as a diversionary force near Santiago de Cuba.

All transports were armed with 12.7mm Browning machine guns and wore Liberian flags.

They were purchased in December 1960 together with two LCIs, named *Barbara J* and *Blagar*, which were to be used as command posts for the invasion. The first was the former LCI 884 of the US Navy, which was later modified as a coastal minesweeper as MHC-28 and later as NRL-28 (Naval Research Laboratory), retired on 18 May 1960 and sold to Mils Marine Company. The *Blagar* cannot be definitely identified, but was also modified into a minesweeper, as it had a crane and space for two boats and could be one of the following: LCI 869 *Gold Crest*, LCI 976 *Ortola* or LCI 515 *Blackbird*, all retired in 1960. They wore Nicaraguan flag and were also armed with 12.7mm machine guns. At least the *Barbara J* and the *Houston* were purchased through the Zapata Offshore Company, the property of George Bush, who suggested the names of the ships, the first after his wife and the other after the city where he lived.

The *Barbara J* continued to serve with the maritime fleet of the CIA under the Mongosse Plan (1962-1965) against Castro under the names *Villaro*, *Explorer* and finally *Petrel*.

The CIA also decided they would need a larger assault ship and landing craft. The first was impossible to get for sale, so it was decided that they would use the USS *San Marcos* (LSD-25), a large landing dock ship built in 1944 and based at Little Creek Amphibious Base. She would carry three LCUs (each armed with two 12.7mm machine guns) that the US Navy sold to the CIA for $125,000 each, carrying the tanks, trucks, jeeps, other vehicles and supplies, and four LCVPs (each armed with a single 12.7mm machine gun). The plan was that the *San Marcos* would rendezvous with the Cuban invasion force in international waters and deploy the landing craft there, so the ship would not enter Cuban waters.

On 23 January 1961, the two LCIs departed for Vieques, in Puerto Rico, for training with the USS *San Marcos* and the landing craft.

The Agency, however, felt that the freighters needed escorts to ensure a safe arrival. Admiral Robert Dennison, Commander-in-Chief of the Atlantic Fleet, offered a group of destroyers and a carrier, known as Task Force Alpha. The Navy formed the squadron in the late 1950s to be the premier anti-submarine warfare (ASW) squadron in the fleet. The squadron consisted of seven destroyers and destroyer escorts, an anti-submarine aircraft carrier, ASW planes such as P-2 Neptunes and at least two submarines. Based at Naval Station Norfolk, the squadron was supposed to get the best of everything in ASW technology.[16]

Admiral Dennison noticed that the task force was scheduled to conduct routine ASW exercises off the coast of Rhode Island in early April 1961, which was about when the Agency wanted to launch the operation. He secretly switched the task force's orders to the Caribbean and ordered them to conduct their exercises in the Tropics.

On 28 March, the *Blagar* and *Barbara J.* departed Stock Island, Key West, Florida, for Puerto Cabezas, arriving on 2 April. Enroute they received a cable directing them, upon arrival at Puerto Cabezas, to assemble and test 36 small boats that were to be used in the upcoming operation. After arrival in Puerto Cabezas, the crews of the two ships carried out this mission, completing it on 10 April. The *Blagar* was given the role of command ship and the mission of landing troops on both Blue and Green Beaches. The *Barbara J.* was to land troops on Red Beach and then patrol to the east to cover the landing areas. Each LCI was armed with eleven 12.7mm Browning machine guns and two 75mm recoilless guns.

With the aim of supporting the invasion after establishing a beachhead, two ships from the United Fruit Company, the *Orotava* and the *La Playa*, were loaded with more supplies in the US and sent to the Caribbean to be on call and arrive at the landing area upon request, but in the end they were not requested and returned with their load.

The Trinidad Plan

The initial plan developed in March 1961 had been to stage the invasion in the vicinity of Trinidad:

Plan for Landing: The landing plan provided for simultaneous landing at first light on D-Day of two reinforced rifle companies of approximately 200 men each over two beaches southwest of Trinidad and the parachute landing of a company of equal strength immediately north of Trinidad. The remainder of the force was to land over one of the two beaches in successive trips of landing craft. Two LCI each mounting eleven 50 caliber machine guns and two 75mm recoilless guns were to provide naval gunfire support at the beaches while the entire fleet of B-26 will start on day D-1 at dawn bombing all Cuban military airfields followed by repeated strikes at dusk of the same day and at first light of D-Day against any airfields where offensive aircraft were yet operational.[17]

Trinidad had the advantage of being very close to the Escambray Mountains, where the counter-revolutionaries were operating, and having only two approaches, one to the west and the other to the east, very easily defendable by the invasion troops. Also, it was a little further from La Habana, had a small airfield and a small harbour.

However, this "Trinidad Plan" was rejected by the Department of State, because, to them, it looked like a Second World War invasion and would be too obviously attributable to the United States. So, on or about 11 March 1961, President Kennedy decided that it should not be executed and that possible alternatives should be studied. According to the new plan, any tactical air operations were to be conducted out of an airfield on Cuba, to which those operations could then be attributed, and the Zapata Peninsula of central Cuba with the new airfield at Playa Girón was chosen.

With the location of the invasion changed, the Agency changed the

The Catalina named "Swan" at Puerto Cabezas.

name of the operation from Operation Trinidad to Operation Zapata. The Agency would later change the name a second time, officially settling on Operation Pluto.

The final landing plan

The town of Playa Girón, which is on the coast of the Bahía de Cochinos (Bay of Pigs), was now to be the centre of the landing area, with the town of Playa Larga at the northern end. There would be three beaches for the landing: Red Beach at Playa Larga, Blue Beach at Girón and Green Beach to the east, on the road to Cienfuegos.

In Playa Girón, the government was finishing a tourist resort comprising 180 small buildings, and expecting to inaugurate it on 20 May.

The plan for Blue Beach called for the landing in four LCVPs of two battalions, the 4th aboard the *Caribe* and the 6th aboard the *Río Escondido*, beginning at approximately 1:00 a.m. on 17 April. The three LCUs would leave the USS *San Marcos* 8km from Blue Beach and land at first light. After the landing at Blue Beach was well underway, the *Blagar* was to come alongside the *Atlántico* and take aboard the 3rd Battalion, and, with one LCVP following, proceed 16 miles east to Green Beach, put the battalion ashore and return to Blue Beach to act as Command Ship and direct the offloading of the cargo ships. Aboard each LCI were arms and ammunition for 1,000 men, plus some resupply ammunition. This was to be on call for the brigade ashore. "The landing at Green Beach was to be conducted as soon as we felt we could leave Blue Beach, but was not expected to be done until after daylight of the 17th."[18]

The reconnaissance of the beach itself and the marking of the landing sites was to be conducted by the Special Demolition Teams. One three-man team was in the *Barbara J.* for Red Beach, with a five-man team for Blue Beach and three-man team for Green Beach aboard the *Blagar*. They were to land as soon as the LCIs arrived in the landing areas and while the LCVPs and small boats were loading the troops. They would have about an hour to perform their missions.

For Red Beach, the plan was that the *Barbara J.* would escort the *Houston*, which held the 2nd and 5th battalions ready to land. This was to be done using 12 small boats on board the *Houston*. It was planned to load each boat with 10 men and their equipment. After this landing was completed, the *Barbara J.* was to escort the *Houston* back to Blue Beach where its cargo was to be offloaded by the LCUs. The *Barbara J.* was then to patrol for 10 miles to the east of Green Beach.

According to the CIA, 500 guerrillas already on the island were to have joined the brigade upon its landing, and another 5,000 would arrive within two days, helping it establish and hold a beachhead for

16 *Task Force Alpha in the Bay of Pigs* by Gordon Calhoun at www.history.navy. mil/museums/hrnm/files/daybook/pdfs/vol9issueone.pdf

17 Record of paramilitary action against the Castro government of Cuba 17 March 1960 – May 1961, Clandestine Services History, written by Colonel J. Hawkins – USMC – 5 May 1961.

18 National Defense University, Taylor Papers, Box 12, Cuba, Paramilitary Study. Secret; Eyes Only.

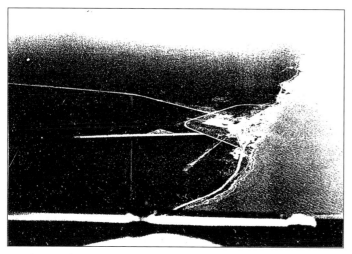

Aerial view of Girón taken from a US spy plane, most probably an RF-101. The airfield is clearly visible to the left.

the three days Castro needed to mount his defence.

In the meantime, paratroopers would have closed off access to the sea at three locations: Horquitas close to Yaguaramas, Jocuma near the Covadonga Sugar Mill and on the road connecting the Australia Sugar Mill and Playa Larga.

The invasion force's planes would destroy the enemy as it tried to reach the brigade at the beachhead. The CIA plan stated: "We'll protect the invasion with an umbrella. The air will belong to us. Every five minutes there will be a plane over all the major roads of Cuba."[19] Once the brigade took Playa Girón, its planes would then destroy all the railroads and bridges "in order to isolate said areas from enemy operations". In a dramatic last-minute assurance, CIA agent Frank Bender announced to the trainees: "We will be there with you for the next step. But you will be so strong; you will be getting so many people to your side, that you won't want to wait for us. You will go straight ahead. You will put your hands out, turn left, and go straight into La Habana."[20]

19 *The Bay of Pigs*, Howard Jones, Oxford University Press, New York, 2008.
20 *The Bay of Pigs*, Howard Jones, Oxford University Press, New York, 2008.

CHAPTER 4
CUBAN REVOLUTIONARY ARMED FORCES

After the revolutionaries achieved power in the country, they reorganized the armed forces completely, despite initially keeping the original set-up. The Cuban Army, which included the Air Force, was called the Ejército Constitucional de Cuba, while the Navy was the Marina de Guerra Constitucional and had a small naval aviation force. Most of the personnel of both forces were removed when the revolutionaries took over the government. Many were imprisoned or executed for their participation in activities against the revolution, and many others managed to escape into exile, leaving only a few personnel who kept working for the new regime.

Ejército Revolucionario
The Cuban Army was created in 1908, and in 1915 was reorganized to include the Guardia Rural paramilitary force, after which it had eight regiments, six of them of cavalry and one each of artillery and infantry, while the Guardia Rural was organized into squadrons.

The Army's organization changed through the years and the force grew in numbers and units, especially after the Second World War, when Cuba took an active part with the allies and received a lot of equipment from the US government under Lend Lease, including the first tanks of the force, eight Marmon-Herrington CTMS 1TB1 light tanks and eight M3A1 White scout cars. By the end of the Second World War, there were ten regiments and the force received many new weapons, including M1 Garand rifles, M2 carbines, M1919 and M2 machine guns, M-20 "Super Bazooka" rocket launchers, more M3A1 scout cars, 24 M3A1 Stuart light tanks, M8 scout cars, a batch of T17 Staghound armoured cars - received from Nicaragua in 1956 - and seven M4 Sherman tanks in 1957.

With the beginning of guerrilla operations against the Batista regime, the Army strength was quickly increased, and by June 1958 reached about 38,000 men, but their morale was very low and they did little to fight the guerrillas, who had a maximum strength of about

One of the seven M4 Sherman tanks of the Cuban Army.

Fifteen Comet tanks were received in 1958 by the Cuban Army and used briefly after the revolution.

Left and right: The frigate *Antonio Maceo* during a visit to New Orleans in 1950.

A ZB-53 7.92mm machine gun used by the Revolutionary Army during the fight at Girón.

The frigate *José Martí* of the US Tacoma class, of the Cuban Revolutionary Navy.

3,000 men in the last days of the struggle. When the US government declared an embargo on weapons sales to the Batista government, the Cubans urgently looked for other suppliers, and by mid-1958 fifteen A34 Comet medium tanks were purchased from the UK, but they did not arrive until December and only saw brief service in the battle at Santa Clara.

When Fidel Castro and his guerrilla comrades assumed power, they abolished Batista's military establishment, transferring its duties to the Ejército Revolucionario, which was soon renamed the Fuerzas Armadas Revolucionarias (FAR, Revolutionary Armed Forces). Some of those who had served in Batista's forces were incorporated into the FAR, but most were released. In October 1959, Fidel Castro created the Ministerio de las Fuerzas Armadas Revolucionarias (MINFAR, Ministry of the Revolutionary Armed Forces), with Raul Castro as its head.

By the end of October 1959, under the auspices of Ernesto "Che" Guevara, the Milicias Nacionales Revolucionarias (MNR, Revolutionary National Militias) were created, with the aim of giving military training to all the population and using them to fight against the growing opposition to the revolution, caused by the new regime's turn towards communism.

Another organization, founded in September 1960, was the Comités de Defensa de la Revolución (CDR, Committees for the Defence of the Revolution), composed of people in every neighbourhood. Originally, the CDR served as local vigilance committees, supporting the security apparatus.

At least five Marmon Herrington, eighteen Stuarts, all the Comets and the seven Shermans were transferred to the Revolutionary Army, but the new government immediately started to look for new equipment, as opposition forces were growing and the relationship with the US was worsening.

Initially, Castro looked for European suppliers and around 24,000 FAL rifles and three batteries of Oto Melara M-56 105mm howitzers, purchased by the Batista government, were delivered just after the rebels siezed power. More Belgian-built weapons were lost with the explosion of the *La Coubre* steamer in La Habana.

By the end of 1959 and early 1960, Castro, with tension increasing with the US, started to negotiate with the Soviet government for the provision of weapons, as he expected a US invasion or US-backed invasion of exiles to happen soon. The Soviet government agreed to support him in April 1960, delivering 100 Czech-built T-34-85 tanks,

The corvette *Siboney* entering La Habana harbour.

The frigate *Máximo Gómez*, sistership of the *José Martí* and *Antonio Maceo*.

The corvette *Siboney*.

The PCE type corvette *Caribe*, sistership of the *Siboney*.

but deliveries were delayed and did not started until October, finishing by December. They were followed by another 25 of a total that reached 205, which arrived before the Bay of Pigs invasion, but by that time the crews had not finished their training at Managua Army Base. The order was later raised to 412, and in the end reached almost 500. One regiment, with about 20 T-34s, was used against the Brigade 2506.

Along with the T-34s, 41 IS-2M heavy tanks were delivered between the end of 1960 and April 1961, equipping two regiments. During the actions of the Bay of Pigs, some were deployed to the Central Australia sugar mill, but were kept in reserve and not used in action.

With the arrival of the new Eastern Bloc tanks, all those surviving from the Batista era were retired.

Together with the tanks, a small quantity of SUU-100 casemate tanks, with 100mm guns, were delivered and used as self propelled artillery by the Cubans. Towed artillery delivered included 122mm guns, BS-3 M-1944 100mm guns and M-1937 152mm guns, along with a big quantity of anti-aircraft guns, especially the Czech 12.7mm M-53 quadruple machine guns, known in Cuba as "Cuatro Bocas" (Four Mouths), and M-1939 37mm guns.

Among the light guns received from the communist bloc were Czech-built Sa.25 9mm sub-machine guns, PPsh-41 7.62 sub-

machine guns, Vz-52 and Vz-57 7.62mm semi-automatic rifles, Ak-47 automatic rifles, ZB-53 7.92mm machine guns, DShKM/Type 54 12.7mm machine guns, M-43 120mm and 82-PM-41 82mm mortars.

By the beginning of 1961, the Revolutionary Army had a strength of about 20,000 men organized into nine light infantry divisions, each consisting of two brigades (which replaced the regiments) of two battalions, nominally of about 900 men each, although most were smaller. Each brigade also had a machine gun unit, an anti-tank battery and a reconnaissance company. The tanks were organized in an armoured division at Managua, and each division had an artillery battalion, an anti-aircraft battery and an armoured company.

Elements of the following are believed to have taken part in the actions at Bay of Pigs:[21]

Army Armoured Division (Managua): tactical force and tank company with T-34-85s and SUU-100s. Artillery: Camagüey Battalion, Batteries 3 and 11 with 122mm guns and 12.7mm and

21 *The Bay of Pigs, Cuba 1961*, Alejandro de Quesada, Osprey Publishing, Oxford, 2009.

Aftermath of the accident involving the rebel Kingfisher serialled 50 at Sierra Maestra.

One of the three Vought Sikorsky OS2U-3 Kingfishers received by the Cuban Navy in 1942.

One of the seven Grumman (General Motors-built) TBM-3S2 Avengers of the Cuban Naval Aviation. Four were transferred to the Fuerza Aérea Revolucionaria in 1960 and used briefly for training.

37mm anti-aircraft guns. Unified Medical Battalion.

From the National Revolutionary Militia, Battalions 26, 113, 114, 116, 117, 120, 123,148, 180, 211, 219, 225, 227, 303 and 339, and Artillery Battery 3 with 122mm field guns. For the militia, the country was divided into three commands, with the battalions from La Habana starting with a '1', those from Matanzas with a '2' and those from Las Villas with a '3'.

Also participating were elements of the Revolutionary National Police Battalion, Revolutionary Militia School auxiliaries and the National Institute of Agrarian Reform (INRA).

Marina Revolucionaria

The Cuban Revolutionary Navy took almost no part in the actions, despite one of its ships, the patrol craft *Baire*, being sunk by B-26s. The Cuban Navy was formally established in 1909 from the Coast Guard that had been operating since 1901. The force had an active participation in the Second World War 2, patrolling the coastal waters against German submarines, and on 15 May 1943, the CS-13 coast guard cutter (one of eight delivered in March of that year) sunk U-*176* in the Florida Strait. The Cuban action had its consequences, and seven months later the *Libertad* transport ship was torpedoed and sunk off the US coast by a U-boat.

Just after the war, three Tacoma class frigates were delivered by the US government - named *José Martí, Antonio Maceo* and *Máximo Gómez* - together with two PCE type corvettes (*Caribe* and *Siboney*),

five SC type submarine chasers (*Oriente, Camagüey, Las Villas, Habana* and *Pinar del Río*) and three US-built Vosper-type PT boats, numbered R 41 to R 43. Two rescue tugs were purchased in the US and received the names *20 de Mayo* and *10 de Octubre,* and the *Leoncio Prado* patrol vessel was finished in La Habana in 1946 as the only member of a planned three-ship class. In the 1950s, 14 minor patrol boats were acquired, together with the US PC type patrol vessel *Baire*. The cruiser *Cuba*, built in 1911, was also still operational.

All these ships were received by the revolutionary government and no additions were made to the fleet before the actions at the Bay of Pigs. The main bases were La Habana, Mariel (to the west of La Habana) and Cayo Loco, in Cienfuegos, while at the time of the invasion the *Baire* was at the small port of Siguanea in Isla de Pinos.

The Navy also had a Naval Aviation force, established in December 1927, which in January of the following year received a Fokker Universal with floats originally purchased by the Cuerpo de Aviación. During the following years, and until the Second World War, the force maintained a minimal air unit with mostly civil types, until in July 1942 receiving three Vought Sikorsky OS2U-3 Kingfishers (serialled 49-51), followed by two Grumman JRF-5 Goose with serials 56 and 57 and at least two Boeing-Stearman N2S-4 Kaydet biplane trainers by March 1943. These were joined by three Naval Aircraft Factory N3N-1 primary trainers in July 1943, accompanied by three Curtiss S03C-2C Seagulls diverted from delivery to Great Britain.

After the Second World War2, the force received two Consolidated PBY-2 Catalinas (serials 70 and 71), allegedly seized from the Caribbean Legion at Cayo Confites in August 1947, augmented in July 1952 by two PBY-5A (one of which was a Boeing Canada-built

A parade in 1953, with six Piper Cubs of the FAEC taxiing at La Habana Malecon (coastal road).

Three of the four B-25H Mitchells, which together with two B-25Cs were the biggest bombers of the FAEC.

A line of Republic P-47D Thunderbolts. The model was used during the operations against the rebels between 1957 and 1959, and very briefly by the FAR.

One of the Curtiss C-46s, serialled 610, of the FAEC.

PB2B-l) serialled 72 and 73. In September 1954, the FAEC's two OA-10 Catalinas (serials 190 and 191) were transferred to the Navy with seven Boeing Stearman N2S-4 Kaydets. In 1952, the force received four new Grumman G-44A Widgeons direct from the manufacturer, and the Naval air arm received its only true combat-capable aircraft under MAP in mid-1956, when seven Grumman (General Motors-built) TBM-3S2 Avengers arrived, serialled 60-66. Finally, although not in fact delivered, two of the five Sikorsky S-55s helicopters purchased for the FAEC were intended for assignment to the Navy.

The Kingfisher serialled 50 was taken by the revolutionaries and used by them on their tiny Fuerza Aérea Revolucionaria during 1958, but was retired shortly after the revolution won.

In 1960, it was decided to disband the Naval Aviation and the remaining aircraft were transferred from their base in Mariel to San Antonio de los Baños. By then, only one Catalina (two were lost in accidents, two were out of service by the end of 1958 and one was left at Mariel out of service in 1960) and four Avengers were operational, and the latter were used until shortly before the Bay of Pigs invasion for advanced training of the first group of 12 cadets being prepared to fly the Sea Furies after flying the Texan. According to General Rafael del Pino, some of the Avengers were damaged in belly landings while training and, most probably, were not repaired. The Catalina was used for maritime patrols until 15 April 1961.

Fuerza Aérea Revolucionaria

The Cuban Military Aviation, named Cuerpo Aéreo del Ejército, was born in May 1913, when a single Curtiss FS was received and started flight activities. The force kept a minimum strength, with two Morane

Saulniers being added, until, on 11 December 1918, a US Aeronautical mission arrived in the country and delivered six Curtiss JN-4D Jennys (serials 1-6) and the Aviation School was organized, also starting flights all over the country. One of the Jennys was lost on 7 July 1919, in what was the first accident of the force, with the loss of the two crewmembers. In that year, the Columbia Airfield was built to the south-west of La Habana, being the first air base in the country.

The fleet was not expanded until mid-1925, when four Vought QO-2 Corsairs (serials 7-11) joined the three surviving Jennys. In the following year, two Corsairs flew to Port au Prince in Haiti in the first international flight of the force. In 1927, the Jennys were retired, being replaced by six de Havilland DH-4M-1s (11-16), received the previous year, while in February 1928, four Consolidated (Buffalo) PT-3 Huskys arrived, followed by another six in 1930, serialled 1-8, 11 and 12. In October 1929, three Curtiss P6S Hawks arrived, followed later by another three, serialled 9, 10 and 15-18. Six Vought O2U-1A Corsairs (19 to 21) were also purchased, followed later by another five (22-26) and three O2U-3As (27-29), and finally by another five O2U-3As with serials up to 34. In 1931, during a revolt at Gibara, the air corps had its baptism of fire, with the loss of a Hawk and two Corsairs. The Hawks 16 and 17 and Corsairs 26, 28, 32 and 33 took part in these actions.

In 1930, the newspaper *El País* donated two Waco 9 (serials 13 and 14) and two Waco 10 planes, but the latter pair were lost before receiving their serials. In 1932, the fleet was augmented with four Curtiss Hawk IIs (19-22) and one Aeronca C-3.

A reorganization of the force took place in 1934, when it was divided into the Army Aviation and Naval Aviation, first with the

On 26 December 1958, the B-26C serialled FAEC-933 flew to Miami, defecting from the Batista government as the pilot rejected orders to attack rebel forces. The same serial was used by the fake defecting plane on 15 April 1961, but in that case the plane was a B-26B.

flying school at Columbia and a fighter and bomber squadron at Campo de Aviación Teniente Brihuegas. No planes were received, but in 1935 a single Waco S3HD-A (serial 23) arrived, along with a Curtiss Robin between October 1935 and September 1937 and a Bellanca Airbus 66-75 (103) from August 1935.

By 1937, attrition was a major issue and the fleet consisted only of the Bellanca, the Waco, four Vought Corsairs and three Curtiss Hawk IIs, while one of the Corsairs was lost in an accident and, on 11 January 1939, the last Hawk, the 21, was lost.

However, in July 1937, the fleet was revived with one Stinson SR-9DD Reliant (104) and five Curtiss CW-19R Hawks (50-54). Two of them were later re-serialled 101 and 102, the first of which was lost in an accident and the other used for ground training at Ceiba del Agua Technical School.

On 12 November 1937, a flight across Latin America, called Pro Faro de Colón, organized with the intention of gathering support for the construction of a monument to remember the arrival of Columbus in America ,was started by the Cuban and Dominican Air Corps, with a single Dominican Curtiss Wright R-19 and three Stinson Reliants, called Santa María, Pinta and La Niña, one belonging to the Air Corps, another to the Naval Aviation and the other being privately owned. They flew from Miraflores in the Dominican Republic to San Juan de Puerto Rico, Caracas (Venezuela), Port of Spain (Trinidad), Paramaribo (Guayana), Belem, Natal, Recife, Bahía, Rio de Janeiro and Porto Alegre in Brazil, Montevideo (Uruguay), Buenos Aires (Aeródromo Militar El Palomar), Santiago de Chile and La Paz (Bolivia). On the flight to Lima, Peru, they lost contact with the La Niña plane, which had to make an emergency landing, but they re-formed later in the Peruvian capital and followed to Bogotá, Colombia.

From there they took off on 29 December, heading to Panamá, but the three Cuban planes crashed into a mountain close to the Cali River while flying through stormy weather, killing all the occupants. The Dominican plane, which was flying behind them, was able to avoid the tragedy.

One year later, the flight was remembered with a flight of the Curtiss CW-19Rs 50, 51 and 52, equipped with extra fuel tanks, to the city of Cali in Colombia.

Growth during the Second World War

In 1939, the Cuerpo de Aviación del Ejército de Cuba was reorganizad into the Escuadrón de Observación y Bombardeo, with five pilotos, and the Escuadrón de Persecución, with another five pilots. Meanwhile, between July 1939 and March 1940, seven Boeing Stearman A73B1s were received, with serials 43 to 49, and in April 1941, four Aeronca 65TCs arrived, which were transferred to the ANACRA (Academia Nacional de Aviación Civil y Reserva Aérea, Air Reserve and Civil Aviation National Academy) to train civil pilots.

When Cuba entered the Second World War, supporting the Allies, it started to receive planes under Lend Lease, starting in 1942 with six Boeing Stearman PT-17 Kaydets (38-43), six Vultee BT-13 Valiants (66-71) and six North American AT-6C Texans (100-105). The next year saw the arrival of the Vultee BT-13s serialled 72-74, AT-6Cs 106-108, Boeing Stearman N2S-4s serialled 44-46 and Aeronca L-3Bs with serials 1-11, the latter for the ANACRA. Six Curtiss Wirght SNC-1 were received on 27 July 1942, which carried serials 55-60, but they were not accepted because the Wirght engine installed wasn't the requested Pratt & Whitney, so they were delivered to Venezuela instead.

In 1945, the Texan fleet was increased with ten AT-6Fs, which received serials 111-120. All the Texans were used on reconnaissance flights along the coast searching for German submarines, despite lacked sufficient capabilities. To increase the air power, four B-25Hs (302-305), two Consolidated Catalinas (190 and 191), two C-47s (200 and 201), one Beech F-2B (photo survey version of the C-45, serialled 212) and one Beech UC-45F (213) were delivered.

The air base of San Antonio de los Baños was built by the US government in 1942 and used by them in anti-submarine operations, followed one year later by the San Julian Naval Air Auxiliary Station, both transferred to the Cuban Army Air Corps in 1945 when the war was over.

San Antonio de los Baños was kept in use, together with Campo Columbia air base, while San Julián remained as a technical school for the Air Corps, but without flying units.

During the war, a civil Beech S.17D Staggerwing (serial 1), a Stinson 105 (serial 2) and a 108 (serial 3) were confiscated, and in 1946 the force started to receive surplus equipment from the US, with one Douglas C-53D (serial 209), eight C-47s (202-211) and, in 1947, two Beech AT-7s (150 and 151), two AT-11s (160 and 161) and six

The Douglas C-47 serialled FAEC-206.

The B-26C serialled FAEC 901 with an unusual black colour scheme. Some Cuban pilots stated there was only one painted in these colours.

Diaz Lanz, on the right, with the T-28A of the Movimiento 26 de Julio.:

Four B-26Cs bound for Cuba embargoed by the US government after the revolution.

The sole T-28A of the Cuban military aviation shortly after the revolution, with the title FAC instead of FAEC or FAR. The plane was purchased in the US and used by the Movimiento 26 de Julio, then transferred to the Rebel Air Force.

Beech 35 Bonanzas (10 to 15).

When, in August 1947, the expedition of the Caribbean Legion organization to invade the Dominican Republic and overthrow President Trujillo was aborted at Cayo Confites, their planes were confiscated by the Cuban government, those being six Lockheed P-38L Lightings (re-serialled 121-126), two Lockheed P-38Ns (127 and 128), one B-24 Liberator (214), two B-25C Mitchells (300 and 301), one C-47 (205), one PB4Y-1 Privateer, one Lockeed Ventura, one C-46 and two Cessna UC-78 Bobcat. Most of them were pressed into service, but in 1948 a hurricane damaged the Liberator, the C-46 and other planes, and the Liberator at least never flew again. The

Lightnings provided an important fighter force for the country, while the Mitchells formed a small but effective medium bomber force.

In 1949, the Air Corps added their first helicopter, a Hiller UH-12, serialled 111, and, in 1950, received two Lockheed C-60A Lodestar (214 and 215), one Lockheed C-56 (with civil serial CU-EDU-1) and one Cessna 190 (CU-EDU-2), followed by two de Havilland Canada DHC-2 Beavers in 1951.

After General Fulgencio Batista's coup d'état in 10 March 1952, the Cuerpo de Aviación was reorganized into the Fuerza Aérea del Ejército de Cuba (FAEC) on 23 April, subordinated to the Army Command. The new force was increased in strength in the same year with 29 Republic F-47D Thunderbolts (450-478), which became the main fighters.

The force continued growing and, in 1953, received seven Piper PA-20 Tri Pacers (serials 1-7) and five PA-18-135 Super Cubs (20-24). Thanks to the support that Batista received from the US government, the force received their first jets in 1954, eight Lockheed T-33s (serials being the odd numbers from 701 to 715) via the Military Assistance Program (MAP). Batista intended to buy jet fighters and he started to negotiate for them. In 1956, the US government offered a batch of F-80 Shooting Stars via MAP, but the increasing internal struggle led to the decision to cancel their delivery.

Meanwhile, in 1954, Batista acquired 16 Douglas B-26C Invaders (serials being the odd numbers from 901 to 931), followed in 1955 by four Piper PA-22-150s (25-28), three PA-22-160s (34-36) and one Aerocommander 560 (128). In 1956, two Bell 47G-2 (serials H-1 and H-2) joined the helicopter fleet, followed in 1957 by a single TB-26C (serial 933), six de Havilland Canada DHC-2 Beavers (15-20) and four Curtiss C-46 Commandos (610-613).

The FAEC during the revolution

When, on 5 September 1957, a revolution attempt was started by the Navy at Cayo Loco Naval Base in Cienfuegos, the P-47s and B-26s were sent to bomb the base and the occupied city, but most of the pilots supported the rebels and dropped their bombs in the sea, causing a purge among pilots when the rebellion was defeated.

The US then declared an embargo on supplying the Batista regime, which had to look for other sources, purchasing a single Douglas C-54 serialled 615 in 1957, followed a year later by three Beavers (29-31), three Westland Whirlwind helicopters (H-9-H-11) and, to replace the P-47s, Batista ordered 15 Hawker FB.11 Sea Furies (serials in multiples of five from 500 to 570; 500, 505, 510 etc.) and two Sea Fury T.20 two-seaters (575 and 580), but the first 10 arrived just a few days before Batista fled the country and were not used in action against the rebels.

Douglas Rudd after his first solo flight on a T-33.

One of the Cuban Mustangs during its brief operational service in the country.

Five of the 10 T-28As purchased by the Batista regime and finally embargoed by the US government.

One of the two Mustangs purchased by the rebels. They arrived late and saw no action during the revolution. They were later used briefly by the FAR. The 401 still survives.

Three of the T-28s embargoed from Cuba at Miami.

Meanwhile, a batch of 10 North American T-28As was purchased in the US and received serials 150-159, together with four additional B-26Cs, but they were embargoed by the US government in Miami and never reached Cuba.

The Rebel Air Force

During the revolutionary war, the Movimiento 26 de Julio organized their small air arm, first using rented transport planes to carry weapons from the US and Central America to the hills in south-east Cuba, and on 12 April 1958, Raúl Castro created the Fuerza Aérea Rebelde with two Piper PA-12s, one Cessna 120 and one Piper Tri Pacer, followed by a Cessna 195 which was lost on its ferry flight from Miami in June. A Beech D-18 carrying weapons was destroyed on the ground by the FAEC on 30 August.

On 10 November, a Naval Aviation Kingfisher was captured when making a forced landing on an airfield controlled by the rebels. The plane received the engine of a Beech 17 Staggerwing that was in the hands of the rebels and out of service to return it into service, being used by Luis Silva Tablada to bomb government forces.

Castro wanted to have his own fighter aircraft, to intercept the FAEC attack planes and attack Cuban Army forces, and the Movimiento 26 de Julio managed to buy three P-51D Mustangs in the US, of which only two arrived in Cuba, having former US civil serials N5422V and N68DR and receiving serials FAR 400 and 401. They were being armed and prepared for action when the revolution ended and were not used in combat.

Meanwhile, on 4 December 1958, a single T-28A purchased in the United States arrived to join the rebels, being the last plane to be enlisted by the tiny air force.

The embargoed T-28A Trojans, with the propellers removed. In the end, the planes never reached Cuba.

The 10 T-28As purchased by Batista were painted with the new FAR markings, but the US government decided not to deliver them, nor the four B-26C Invaders.

A parade of the Milicias Revolucionarias created by the new government after the revolution to increase Cuban military power when activities against the revolution increased.

Fuerza Aérea Revolucionaria

As soon as the rebel forces took control of the country, the Air Force, like all the Cuban armed forces, underwent a purge, in which all Batista supporters were ousted, especially those who took part in the attacks on the guerrillas. The force's operational status soon became extremely poor. Only a handful of pilots and mechanics remained on duty, most of them being those who were prosecuted after the failed coup attempt of 1957 or who were part of the Rebel Air Force. Pedro Luis Díaz Lanz, a rebel pilot dedicated to carry weapons from the US, was appointed commander of the new Fuerza Aérea Revolucionaria (FAR, Revolutionary Air Force) and the decision was taken to start training new pilots. The force was organized with the few pilots remaining (including Silva Tablada, Enrique Carreras Rolas, Álvaro Prendes, Guillermo Figueroa, Douglas Rudd, Alberto Fernández and Gustavo Bourzac) and a few guerrilla soldiers with some flight experience, such as Rafael del Pino.

To help train the new crews, a group of nine Chilean pilots and mechanics was hired, including Jaques Lagas, but when Castro started to move the country towards socialism, all except Lagas returned to Chile. Meanwhile, Nicaraguan pilots Carlos Ulloa, Alvaro Galo and Ernesto Guerrero joined the FAR after being exiled from their country for taking part in a rebellion against President Somoza.

The force kept its headquarters at Columbia air base, now renamed Libertad, and San Antonio de los Baños, using other airports around the country for deployments.

The FAEC planes were also merged with those of the FAR and, later, by the surviving two Catalinas and four Grumman TBM Avengers of the Naval Aviation.

Meanwhile, on 28 June 1959, Díaz Lanz was replaced as commander of the force by Comandante Juan Almeida Bosque.

The FAR was divided into the Escuadrón de Persecución y Combate - with the Furies, T-33s, the two Mustangs and the remaining P-47s - the Escuadrón de Bombardeo - with the Invaders - the Escuadrón de Transporte - with the C-47s, C-54s and C-46s - which had a training escadrille added, with the Texans, and the sole T-28 and a liaison escadrille with Piper PA-22s. The Escuadrón de Enlace had all the small planes, such as the Beavers and a small fleet of Pipers and Cessnas. The Avengers were also used as advanced trainers, as the single T-28 wasn't enough and the new pilots needed a transitional plane between the Texans and Sea Furies.

The remaining 10 P-47s and the two Mustangs saw little service after the revolution as priority was given to the Sea Furies and T-33s, and there were not enough budget, nor mechanics nor pilots, for all of them. The Thunderbolts and Mustangs were all out of service by the time of the Bay of Pigs invasion.

The seven Sea Furies that had not arrived before the fall of Batista were delivered early in 1959, together with most of their weapons, including bombs and 297 HVAR rockets.

The Cuban government was negotiating with Hawker for the provision of an extra batch of 10 Sea Furies, and Castro asked if they could be changed for a batch of Hawker Hunters, but US pressure on the British government prevented this from happening. The refusal by the British to deliver the Hunters was one of the reasons that Castro approached the Soviet government for the provision of fighters, with a first order for a batch of 24 MiG-15s and four MiG-15UTIs. Cuban pilots were sent to Czechoslovakia to be trained, but the planes did not arrive at San Antonio de los Baños until 6 June 1961 and the pilots returned on March 1962, after the actions at the Bay of Pigs.

The period between 1 January 1959 and the Bay of Pigs was one of a tiny force trying to train new pilots and mechanics as fast as possible, while also trying to maintain the planes in the best operational status and be ready for war, as the increasing activities of dissidents and tension with the United States were seen as signals that an invasion would follow sooner or later. This situation led to an increase in accidents rates, with the loss of the T-33 serialled 701, seven Sea Furies, two Avengers, two C-47s, one PA-22, one Beaver and one Cessna 310 (a civilian one pressed into service with the FAR).

According to Rafael del Pino,[22] by 15 April 1961 there were ten F-47s out of service, two Mustangs also out of service, five FB.11 Sea Furies, six B-26Cs (but with only Captain Silva Tablada, Chilean Captain Jackes Lagas and Nicaraguan 1st Lieutenant Álvaro Galo as pilots), five T-33s (703, 707, 709, 711 and 715), seven Texans, the sole T-28, two C-47s, one C-46, one Catalina and one C-54 (baptized *Cuatro Vientos*). There were also some liaison airplanes, and three Bell 47s and one Westland Whirlwind helicopters. Some sources indicate at least one TBM operational, but Del Pino stated that none of them were in service by April 1961.

The condition of almost all aircraft was very poor, and the T-33

22 Email to the author

serialled 703 was out of service, being repaired during the action. The engines were in very bad condition and the pilots often had to make emergency landings.

To increase the capability of the T-33 for air combat, work was started using the nose of the 701, lost in a take-off accident, to install four 7.62mm machine guns, but they were not ready when the invasion was defeated, and the arrival of the MiGs after the invasion put an end to this scheme.

The Sea Furies received a new paint scheme, with camouflage of dark green and brown on the upper part and light blue on the lower. Some sources also state that some planes were serialled 541, 542 and 543, which could mean a change of serials, but this cannot be corroborated. The preserved planes used these serials, but there are no pictures from the time of Bay of Pigs in which the existence of those serials could be checked.

By the time of the Bay of Pigs invasion, the pilots prepared to fly combat aircraft were Silva Tablada (only on B-26), Enrique Carreras Rolas (B-26, T-33 and Sea Fury), Álvaro Prendes (T-33 and Sea Fury), Guillermo Figueroa (T-33 and Sea Fury), Douglas Rudd (T-33 and Sea Fury), Alberto Fernández (T-33 and Sea Fury), Gustavo Bourzac (Sea Fury), Rafael del Pino (T-33 and Sea Fury), Jaques Lagas (B-26), Carlos Ulloa (Sea Fury), Alvaro Galo (B-26) and Ernesto Guerrero (T-33 and Sea Fury).

CHAPTER 5
FIRST AIR STRIKES

The plan

The initial operations plan for the airstrikes against Cuba prior to D Day, called Operation Puma, aimed at the total destruction of the FAR on the ground. Due to the lack of fighters, with only light anti-aircraft defences on the ships and no protection on the B-26s (the two defensive turrets of the planes were removed to reduce weight and increase range), it was considered too great a danger to leave the FAR fighters and B-26s operational. The plan also called for attacks on some ground forces, tactical targets close to the landing area, military depots and other targets.

The plan was to carry out a series of large air strikes from D-2 until D Day, with two air strikes per day – one at dawn and the other at dusk - using as many aircraft as possible, with those on D Day dedicated to attacking targets around the landing area and providing close air support. It was also planned to deploy at least two B-26s to Playa Girón airfield to support plausible deniability regarding US responsibility for the attacks, and also to protect the invading Brigade. This forced a change in the cargo to be carried on the landing vessels, as they had to add the ground support equipment for the planes.

The size and quantity of the air strikes planned, however, made the CIA Deputy Director (Plans) worry that they could not deny their participation in such a large-scale operation, so he called for a reduction in its size. Only one attack on D-3 was authorized, and with only six planes, two to Ciudad Libertad Air Base, two to San Antonio de los Baños and two to Santiago de Cuba's Antonio Maceo airport. Finally, after a meeting at Puerto Cabezas on 9 April, the quantity was later raised to eight planes, with the attacks on the first two targets both conducted by three planes. This change to the plans, reducing the attack force, was one of the main causes of the failure of the whole invasion, as it wasn't possible to destroy all of the FAR on the ground

and its planes would pose the most serious threat to the operation.

Also, a ninth plane was to receive shots to its engine panels and fuselage (with light weapons), fly directly to Miami and land, with the pilot saying he was a defecting Cuban pilot and that a rebellion had started among the air force. This was to create the idea that the operation was in fact an uprising by Castro's Armed Forces and not an exiles invasion.

A tenth airplane was prepared as an airborne backup in case one of those going to bomb Cuba suffered a failure and could not perform the mission.

The selection of the targets was made using the best available Lockheed U-2 photography of the three Cuban airfields that had been taken on 11 and 13 April 1961.

According to the CIA:

On 13 April, there were five B-26s and five F-47s or Sea Fury aircraft at Campo Libertad. At San Antonio de los Baños, on the same date, there were at least five B-26s, one T-33, and one F-47 or Sea Fury - the readout, however, noted that haze and partial cloud cover had obscured most of the San Antonio airfield. The Santiago airfield had been photographed on 11 April, and there were two B-26s, one T-33, and one derelict F-47 or Sea Fury aircraft identified on the photography. In addition to the aircraft at Libertad, at least 140 trucks and 130 pieces of artillery were identified on the infield between the runways and taxiways.[23]

There were usually no planes based at Santiago de Cuba, but in early April it was decided to send a small force there, comprising the T-33

23 *Official history of the Bay of Pigs Operation*, Jack Pfeiffer, Central Intelligence Agency, 1979.

The plane used as a fake defector, after landing in the United States. Shortly after, it was found that the plane was of a different model than the one in use by the FAR.

One of the FAL's B-26 Invaders, armed with rockets and equipped with extra fuel tanks, as they operated over Bay of Pigs. The plane is seen at Happy Valley. Photo: CIA.

serialled 707 with pilot Orestes Acosta, two B-26s under command of Álvaro Galo and the last operational Catalina with pilot Aldo Losano.

On the night of 14 April, the *Santa Ana*, which was supposed to make a diversionary landing in the Oriente, had been spotted by coast-watchers. After dark, Captain Orestes Acosta was ordered to fly a patrol to try to spot the ship. It should have been done by the Catalina but the pilots were not night-qualified. Acosta took off and soon returned, as Santiago was only a few minutes' flying time from where the *Santa Ana* was located. He called on the radio and asked that the Catalina be prepared for take-off at first light, but shortly after he crashed in the ocean south of Santiago at around 1:00 a.m. on April 15 while preparing to land.

At first light, a FAR C-47 was sent to patrol and search for the T-33, and the attack occurred while the C-47 was flying.

To replace his loss, Douglas Rudd was ordered to deploy on a T-33 from San Antonio de los Baños during 15 April, after the attack, but due to the lack of T-33s he was sent on a Sea Fury.

This left three T-33s (709, 711 and 715), four Sea Fury, three B-26s, three C-47s and smaller planes at San Antonio de los Baños.

According to the CIA:

There also was a deception aspect built into the planned attack on the Libertad and San Antonio airfields. Two of the three B-26s assigned to Libertad and two of the three assigned to San Antonio would bear identical tail numbers. At each airfield, two aircraft with unidentical tail numbers would make the first strikes, and then the third aircraft - with an identical tail number to one of the other aircraft - would make its pass. The theory was that this would make the Cubans believe that a total of only four aircraft were engaged in the strike at San Antonio and Libertad. In fact, this proved to be the case at least for a few days: for Castro, in his 23 April 1961 TV spectacular on the invasion, specified that there had been two aircraft at each of the three airfields.[24]

US Navy and USAF planes flying over the area were informed they had to stay clear of Cuban and Nicaraguan air space, while Nicaraguan Air Force P-51 Mustangs were alerted to intercept any non-scheduled aircraft approaching Happy Valley.

On 13 April, the final orders were received and the escadrilles were organized as follows:

24 *Official history of the Bay of Pigs Operation*, Jack Pfeiffer, Central Intelligence Agency, 1979.

Escadrille Puma, with leader Captain José Crespo and Lorenzo Pérez Lorenzo on plane 933, wingman 1 with Captain Daniel Fernández Mon and Gastón Pérez on plane 935, and wingman 2 with Captain Osvaldo Piedra and José Fernñandez on the 931. Their mission was to attack Ciudad Libertad.

Escadrille Linda, with leader Captain Luis Cosme and Nildo Batista on plane 935, wingman 1 with Captain René García and Luis Ardois on plane 931, and wingman 2 with Captain Alfredo Caballero and Alfredo Maza on another 935, having San Antonio de los Baños as their target.

Escadrille Gorila, with leader Captain Gustavo Ponzoa and Rafael García Pujol on plane 923, and wingman with Captain Gonzalo Herrera and Ángel López on the 929, with Santiago de Cuba airfield as their target.

Meanwhile, Mario Zuñiga had the mission to fly with a plane serialled 933 from Happy Valley to Miami to simulate defection from the FAR.

The backup plane, also with serial 935, was crewed by Raúl Vianello and Demetrio Pérez.

The order was to take off at 2:00 a.m. on 15 April and head for Cuba, each plane armed with ten 250lb or six 500lb bombs, eight HVAR 127mm rockets and 260 shots for each of the eight machine guns.

The 15 April air strike

At 12:30 a.m., the brigade's Catalina took off to act as SAR plane and relay transmissions between the planes and Happy Valley. Later on, the eight planes that were to perform the bombing took off at the planned time and each escadrille headed for their target, but the spare plane had to abort due to a failure in one engine, stopping at the end of the runway.

By that time, with a difference of one hour between Nicaragua and Cuba, when they took off it was 3:00 a.m. Cuban time and 2:00 a.m. at Happy Valley.

All the planes reached Cuba at low altitude at first light, making navigation difficult due to mist. Approaching their targets, they climbed to 3,000ft to start a 40° dive.

The first escadrille to arrive at its target was the Gorila flight, over Santiago de Cuba. The only account of the bombing was what Gonzalo Herrera told Eduardo Ferrer, who published it in his book *Operación Puma*. He explained that arriving at Jamaica, they made a circle, as they were going faster than expected, and then continued as low as they could, to avoid any possible detection. Arriving at the coast, they saw a Cuban Navy patrol boat, which immediately informed the airport of the incoming attack. At 5:55 a.m.,they started the bombing, first against two anti-aircraft artillery (AAA) positions, while the occupants of another two positions abandoned them when they saw the planes aiming at them. Herrera then turned towards the sea to prepare for another pass. Ponzoa, in the meantime, dropped his bombs on the tarmac, destroying a Cubana de Aviación Douglas DC-3 (serial CU-T-172) and the last surviving Catalina of the FAR. Herrera then dropped his bombs over the runway, destroying the fuel depot; at that moment his left engine was hit, but the plane kept flying normally. Meanwhile, Ponzoa destroyed a B-26. On a third pass, Herrera fired his rockets and machine guns against an AAA position, followed by another attack on th runway with his last rockets and then a strafing pass against the AAA. After 20 minutes over the target, Ponzoa called Herrera to say they must return, as they were out of ammunition.

Herrera returned with his hydraulic system severely damaged and had to land with almost no brakes, using the entire runway. They had also destroyed a Sea Fury and an Aerocommander used by Raúl Castro, while damaging another Cubana de Aviación DC-3.

The Puma escadrille appeared over Ciudad Libertad, where there were no serviceable planes, only a few B-26s and F-47s out of service, but as it was the headquarters of the FAR, there was a large concentration of AAA. The attackers managed to destroy some vehicles and depots, but the planes of Crespo and Fernández Mon were seriously damaged; the first headed to Boca Chica at Key West, while the latter was hit on its third pass and exploded, crashing into the sea to the north of La Habana. Fernández Mon and Gastón Pérez were thus the first exiles to die in combat.

The Linda escadrille arrived over San Antonio de los Baños and René García started the attack against a line of between eight and 10 planes, releasing his bombs, despite heavy fire from the ground artillery. He then fired his rockets and machine guns against the battery that was closest to him, destroying it, and headed back to the tarmac, firing the remaining rockets and machine guns against a T-33 and two B-26s. At the same time, Alfredo Caballero started his attack, immediately followed by Luis Cosme. After all planes had fired their weapons, Cosme ordered their return, but Caballero, whose extra fuel tanks were not transferring fuel, headed to Grand Cayman, as he hadn't enough fuel to reach Happy Valley. The crew was then taken by plane to the US and on to Retalhuleu, where they stayed until the end of the action. The plane was recovered by US crews and returned to Happy Valley. Linda had destroyed the T-33 serialled 715, a C-47, one Texan and one F-47, the last being out of service and used as a decoy. One B-26 out of service was also damaged.

The only attempt to intercept the bombers took place at San Antonio de los Baños, where almost all pilots were concentrated. Initially, Enrique Carreras Rolas went to the T-33 715, but the plane was destroyed when he was approaching. After seeing this, Alberto Fernández, who ran to the planes as fast as he could from his house and was only wearing his flying suit - without shoes or underwear - went to another T-33 and started the engine, moving onto the runway. Meanwhile, Gustavo Bourzac, who ran from his house to the base wearing only shorts, went to a Sea Fury and took off after Fernández, but they weren't able to find the B-26s, which departed the area just before they took off. Fernández flew to the south of the island, reaching the Isla de Pinos, where the weather was better, with no clouds. He expected to find the B-26s there, as he was flying faster, but in the end found nothing and had to return. Bourzac tried to find a B-26 that hid in the clouds, but he headed north, supposing the planes were coming from the US. He eventually almost reached Key West before turning

FAR markings and the blue stripe under the wing of a FAL B-26 at Happy Valley. Photo: CIA.

One of the Catalinas used by the FAR. The last operational plane of the model was destroyed during the bombings of 15 April.

back to base, where he asked for clothes before leaving his plane!

Damage assessment

The analysis of 15 April 1961 photography taken by U-2s revealed that the air strikes against the air fields at Campo Libertad, San Antonio de los Baños and Santiago de Cuba made

> … no damage to any of the runways and only minimal apparent damage to the combat aircraft was observed. The only confirmed damage to combat aircraft was the destruction of a B-26 [the FAR 901] at Santiago de Cuba. A C-47 cargo plane [from Cubana de Aviación] and another unidentified probable cargo plane were also destroyed at Santiago de Cuba [in fact it was the Catalina]. A C-47 cargo plane was destroyed at San Antonio de los Baños airfield. The edge of a taxiway was cratered at Campo Libertad airfield. There could have been additional damage to aircraft from cannon fire that would not be visible on the photography. The combat aircraft at Campo Libertad Airfield on 15 April 1961 consisted of four B-26 and five F-47/Sea Fury aircraft. All of these aircraft were parked in out of the way areas, rather than in the main operations area of the airfield and were probably unserviceable. No movement of these aircraft was observed between 11 and 20 April 1961.[25]

At Santiago de Cuba, a FAR Aerocommander used by Raúl Castro was also destroyed, and a second B26 (the FAR 935) was slightly damaged. Despite this, after the planes arrived back at Happy Valley, they received the news that the US government had decided that the

25 *Official history of the Bay of Pigs Operation*, Jack Pfeiffer, Central Intelligence Agency, 1979

The DC-3 serialled CU-T-172 of Cubana de Aviación destroyed at Santiago de Cuba in the bombing of 15 April.

afternoon strike and the two strikes for 16 April were cancelled, and no other operations would take place until the landing.

This was a major frustration for the crews and all the Cubans, as well as the US head in Happy Valley, as they realized they had not destroyed the FAR and that they needed total control of Cuban air space to be successful in the invasion.

Despite what the U-2 photos showed, the combat mission report prepared on 15 April by Colonel Stanley Beerli following the action, and based on the crew reports, stated:[26]

Santiago de Cuba: Both aircraft returned to base safely. Pilots reported airfield completely destroyed and fires everywhere. One B-26 reported destroyed by rockets, one T-33 probably destroyed by .50 caliber fire, and one C-47 destroyed by .50 caliber fire. All aircraft on ramp reported afire. AAA reported as heavy and determined. Aircraft repeatedly exchanged fire with AAA positions until AAA ceased. One aircraft returned base with numerous holes, complete hydraulic failure, and one hung rocket. However, it landed without incident.

San Antonio: Two aircraft returned base safely and pilots reported attack destroyed 75 percent of field. Operations building was destroyed and one T-33 on alert exploded. Two additional T-33s were possibly destroyed. Smoke from bombs partially obliterated target and precluded accurate damage assessment. Heavy AAA was reported. One aircraft landed at Grand Cayman Island because of low fuel.

Libertad: One aircraft returned to base safely and pilot reported target partially destroyed. All bombs fell within confines of the base. (Press reports stated one bomb scored direct hit on an Air Force ammunition dump and explosions were still occurring 30 minutes after the attack.) Heavy AAA was reported. One aircraft was damaged by AAA and forced to feather engine which was on fire. Companion aircraft accompanied toward Key West, but observed damaged aircraft in uncontrolled crash into ocean. No parachutes or survivors were observed. Second aircraft, now low on fuel, continued to Florida and landed at Boca Chica. Extent of damage not yet determined.

Special Aircraft: The special aircraft landed at destination as planned.

Airborne Spare: One airborne spare aircraft aborted on take off [sic], due to engine trouble.

26 *Official history of the Bay of Pigs Operation*, Jack Pfeiffer, Central Intelligence Agency, 1979

The "defecting" plane

Carrying out what was called in code Operation JMFury, Mario Zuñiga flew alone with his plane, taking off at 4:00 a.m. and heading for Cuba. Flying at only 300ft over the island, he passed close to the town of Sancti Spíritus and then headed to Florida, dropping the bombs over the sea to make apparent the plane was armed. At 8:21 a.m., he landed at Miami airport, with Zuñiga declaring he was part of a revolt against Castro and that he had defected after bombing San Antonio de los Baños, with two of his comrades having attacked Ciudad Libertad Air Base. His story did not survive long, as when the US ambassador to the UN showed a picture of the plane, denying any US participation in the actions, observers noted that the plane was a B-26B instead of the B-26Cs used by the FAR, lacked the turrets and was in natural-metal finish, while the FAR ones were grey. Also, the press in Miami realized that the plane which landed at Boca Chica was wearing the same serial (933) as the "defecting" one.

Zuñiga returned to Happy Valley from Opa-Locka on a C-54 that had previously been sent, and also took back the crew of the 933 plane that had landed at Boca Chica - Captain José Crespo and Lorenzo Pérez Lorenzo. Zuñiga's plane was later sent to Eglin AFB and then to Davis-Monthan AFB for storage.

Another defection operation planned, but not carried out, was to fly over La Habana with USAF planes at supersonic speeds to create sonic booms on the night of 14-15 April, creating confusion and more distraction to Castro's forces.

Waiting for more action

After the attacks on the afternoon 15 April and the whole of 16 April were cancelled, the crews spent the rest of the day and the next repairing their planes and analyzing the results of the actions. The force had been left with 12 B-26s, as two were in Florida, one at Grand Cayman and one was shot down. The one at Grand Cayman and that which landed at Boca Chica returned to Puerto Cabezas on 16 April.

The bombing finally alerted Castro that an invasion was imminent. His first decision was to order a huge operation against resistance organizations within the country, detaining about half a million people who were seen as potential supporters of the exile force.

After the attack, all remaining operational combat planes of the FAR were gathered at San Antonio de los Baños, dispersed and placed close to the end of the base's three runways, with the pilots staying on the base and sleeping under their wings, ready to depart in case of a new attack.

On 16 April, the seven men killed in the attack on Ciudad Libertad were taken to La Habana for a mass burial, with Fidel Castro leading the ceremony. To protect the ceremony and prevent an air strike, one

T-33, two Sea Furies and one B-26 flew over the city.

At San Antonio de los Baños, the FAR put the T-33 711 on alert, together with two Sea Furies (armed with rockets and bombs to prevent a landing) and one B-26. There was also the T-33 709, while mechanics started to work to make the 703 operational.

During 16 April, Radio Swan and another 11 radio stations controlled by the CIA began a mass propaganda campaign, including coded orders for resistance groups inside Cuba, but they couldn't fulfill any of their planned actions due to the activities of the Cuban government against them. Also, in what was another of the main failures of the CIA, the agency failed to alerted either the potent and widespread anti-Castro underground or the men from Brigade 2506 who had earlier infiltrated the island. They were left ignorant of the location or date of the attack, without instructions to carry out sabotage or mobilize their ranks to contribute in any way to the operation[27].

___

27 *The Bay of Pigs, Cuba 1961*, Alejandro de Quesada, Osprey Publishing, Oxford, 2009.

CHAPTER 6
INVASION

Assembling the invasion force

While the Brigade 2506 ships were gathering at Puerto Cabezas, on 5 April the US Navy Task Force Alpha departed with the USS *Essex* aircraft carrier - empty of aircraft - escorted by the destroyers USS *Beale, Eaton, Conway, Cony, Murray, Bache* and *Wailer*, with diesel power submarine USS *Cobbler*, the helicopter carrier USS *Boxer* (with about 2,000 Marines on board) and the landing ship USS *San Marcos*. Their crews didn't know about their mission and events became even more mysterious for them when the order went out that the ships' hull numbers were to be painted over and the National Ensign burned, with the tattered remains then reflown. Sailors were told if they had civilian clothes on board, they were to wear them.

The rules of engagement for Operation Bumpy Road, as the Joint Chiefs somewhat ironically called the Navy's involvement in the invasion, were strict, and described in Operation Order 25-61, Annex A, and Appendix I to Annex A, stating that "U.S. Naval vessels and aircraft will not enter Cuban Territorial Waters or airspace (three-mile limit)." The destroyers assigned to provide area coverage of the Cuban Exile Force (CEF) would avoid overt association with the CEF ships, would not be used to support the landing operation and would not close within 20 miles of the objective area.

Outside Cuban Territorial Waters, if intervention by US forces was required to protect the CEF ships from surface attack or to prevent their capture, US forces would intervene as necessary to protect the CEF ship(s). This intervention would cancel the landing operation.

US forces would open fire only if a CEF ship(s) was attacked. After the rendezvous of CEF ships at Point Zulu on D-1 Day, and until the convoy had moved to a point within 20 miles of the objective area, a destroyer commanding officer would place his ship between the convoy and any suspicious or Castro surface craft sighted.

The Combat Air Patrols (CAP) will be stationed so that it will not appear to be covering the CEF ships. Air rules of engagement are as follows:

Any unidentified aircraft approaching within radar range of CEF ships and closing will be investigated.

If investigation reveals the aircraft to be Castro's, the investigating aircraft will make successive close passes ensuring that the Castro aircraft is aware of his presence.

If Castro aircraft maintains course to close CEF ship(s), CAP will continue to make close passes in an attempt to divert.

If Castro aircraft commences firing on the CEF ship(s) or opens its bomb bays and commences a bomb run, CAP will open fire.

Twelve Douglas A-4B Skyhawks from squadron VA-34 Blue Blasters out of Ciecel Field then rendezvoused and trapped aboard *Essex* when the ships passed near Jacksonville.

Meanwhile, at Puerto Cabezas, the briefing team from Washington arrived on 11 April and briefings were conducted on 12, 13 and 14

A view of the pier at Puerto Cabezas, Nicaragua, from where the invasion departed.

The *Houston* loading material in Puerto Cabezas, Nicaragua.

The *Barbara J.* LCI.

The *Blagar* leaving Puerto Cabezas heading for Bahía de Cochinos.

The *Blagar*, one of the two LCIs used as command posts.

The *Río Escondido* anchored in front of Puerto Cabezas pier.

April for the final plans for the invasion, while on the last day the troops gathered on the pier to board the ships, which were loaded over the previous days with all the equipment for the landing force. Only the vehicles were not loaded, as they were all on the USS *San Marcos*.

To bid farewell to the troops, Nicaraguan President Luis Somoza travelled to Puerto Cabezas and declared to the troops boarding the ships: "Bring me some hair from Castro's beard!" The brigade commander and staff were aboard the *Blagar*.

As the *Río Escondido* had damaged her props on logs coming out of New Orleans enroute to Puerto Cabezas, and could only do five knots, this ship was loaded first and had left Puerto Cabezas on 12 April.

The two LCIs and the *Atlántico* had, in total, arms, field equipment and ammunition for outfitting guerrilla forces that were expected to join Brigade 2506, with equipment for 4,000 men, while the latter also carried 10 aluminum boats for the landing. On the USS *San Marcos*, there were seven trucks full of ammunition to be landed with the first LCUs, together with the M-41 tanks, four jeeps, the aviation fuel tanker truck, the water trailer, a D-6 tractor and a tractor crane. The *Río Escondido* was carrying supplies for 10 days of operations, five REO trucks, one jeep, three trailers, a water trailer, a fork lift and a communications trailer. The ship was also carrying ammunition for the planes that would operate from Girón airfield, including 700 HVAR 127mm rockets, 500 fragmentation bombs, 1½ tons of white phosphorous and 20 tons of 12.7mm ammunition.

The *Houston* was carrying eight aluminum boats for the landing, a 50-bed hospital complete with all the medical equipment, fuel, ammunition and 3,660 "C rations" (emergency rations for three days for one soldier).

The *Caribe* was carrying six aluminum boats, food, ammunition and 15 days' supply of aviation ordnance.

The *Lake Charles* was expected to arrive in the area on D Day +

2 with another 10 days of supplies, including six aluminum boats, six jeeps, six trailers and a fork lift. The *Orotava*, which would be on call in the Caribbean Sea, would be carrying supplies for another 20 days and fuel and ordnance for the operation of the Fuerza Aérea de Liberación for 30 days. The load included two extra REO trucks and six aluminum boats. The *La Playa* was also on call, with supplies for 15,000 men, including eight jeeps and ten REO trucks, medical and communication equipment. Finally, the *Orotava* and *La Playa* took no part in the operation.

The *Santa Ana* was carrying supplies for a small diversionary force and six aluminum boats.

On the night of 14 April, all the ships at Puerto Cabezas left the harbour and proceeded independently to an assembly area, where they rendezvoused with a pre-assigned destroyer from Task Force Alpha, which started to escort the transports, keeping their distance from the freighters during the daytime and only closing in at night.

During 16 April, the troops got prepared for the landing and received information on where the landing would take place. They also put on their combat uniforms and checked their weapons. At 5:30 p.m., the ships arrived on station 30 miles off the Cuban coast, and then a column headed by the *Blagar*, followed at 800-yard intervals by the *Caribe*, *Atlántico*, *Barbara J.*, *Houston* and *Río Escondido*, started the approach to the beach. At 8:00 p.m., five miles from Blue Beach, the USS *San Marcos* rendezvoused to deploy the LCUs and LCVPs.

The USS *Essex* waited on standby about 125 miles offshore. The carrier's air wing was augmented by two A-1 Skyraiders which

The *Atlántico* before the invasion.

The *Barbara J.* at Puerto Cabezas.:

flew in from USS *Independence*. The landing force was escorted by the destroyers USS *Murray* and *Eaton*. Once they reached Cuban territorial waters, the American warships withdrew to refuel from the USS *Elokomin*.

Even though the American forces were supposed to be incognito, Admirals Burke and Dennison still wanted to be prepared for the worst. Unknown to all in the task force, the two admirals placed several assets on standby, including a Marine brigade landing team, two more squadrons of destroyers and a Norfolk-based battlegroup that included the aircraft carrier USS *Independence* and cruiser USS *Galveston*, should more firepower be authorized or if Castro decided to make a move against US forces at Guantanamo Bay.[28]

Twenty-foot landing boats on the deck of the *Barbara J.*

Blue Beach

According to a report by Grayston Lynch (a retired US Army Special Forces officer in charge of the frogmen that marked the landing place at Red Beach):[29]

At this point the *Barbara J.* and the *Houston* left the column and proceeded toward Red Beach. The *Blagar* moved on up to within two miles of Blue Beach to launch the underwater demolition teams (UDT). This five-man team and Mr Lynch departed the *Blagar* at 23:45 hours 16 April in a seven-man, Navy rubber UDT boat with a 16 HP silent motor. Two men were armed with BARs (M1918 Browning Automatic Rifle) and the other four with Thompson sub-machine guns. The team was equipped with a PRC-10 radio and lighting sets for beach and buoys for marking the channels. Escorting them part of the way was a 20-foot catamaran boat from the *Blagar*. This boat also had a PRC-10 radio and mounted one .50 (12.7mm) and one .30 (7.62mm) caliber machine gun. This boat was to lie off the beach and provide cover for the UDT teams.

Originally, the submarine USS *Threadfin* was to carry the teams in, but the CIA agent turned out to be claustrophobic. They were finally taken to the *Blagar* on board the destroyer USS *Eaton*. This group of men was the first to land at Bay of Pigs. According to Lynch, the town of Playa Girón was well lit; a cluster of very bright lights to the right of the town proved to be from the small group of buildings at the jetty which marked the right-hand boundary of the landing area.

Grayston Lynch stated in his report:

---

28 *Task Force Alpha in the Bay of Pigs* by Gordon Calhoun at www.history.navy. mil/museums/hrnm/files/daybook/pdfs/vol9issueone.pdf

29 National Defense University, Taylor Papers, Box 12, Cuba, Paramilitary Study. Secret; Eyes Only. Lynch prepared the report for the investigative committee chaired by General Taylor.

Four C-46s and one C-54 at Puerto Cabezas airfield.

Five B-26Bs at Puerto Cabezas airfield

Three abandoned LCVPs at the end of the actions. Two were lost due to the coral reefs on the beaches at Girón.

At about 1,000 yards out, six men were observed outside these buildings looking seaward. As there were no lights or noise from the ships it was assumed that they were merely coast watchers which later checking proved to be correct. The UDT team started into the beach about 300 yards west of these buildings and when 500 yards out, all the lights in the buildings were switched off. The UDT team discovered a coral ridge about 100 yards from the beach running across the front of the landing area and one foot below the surface. They crossed this and started the boat into the beach. Fifty yards from shore a jeep came from the town down the beach road, and headed east and picked them up in its headlights. This jeep stopped directly in front of the team and turned toward the water throwing its headlights on the boat. It then caught the full fire of two BARs and four Thompsons and was knocked out instantly.

The jeep was commanded by Mariano Mustelier, the leader of the militia unit in the town, who was accompanied by Valerio Rodríguez, a teacher who was only 13 years old, the latter being wounded by the bullets. Mustelier made his escape and ordered a man to go to Covadonga and inform La Habana.

The UDT team moved onto the beach and called the *Blagar* on the radio to tell them what had happened, and called for an immediate landing of troops before the enemy could send reinforcements. The team placed a red light by the jeep, moved toward the jetty 150 yards to the east and placed the other one there; then moved out onto the jetty and placed the large white light to guide in the landing craft. While this was happening, someone pulled the master switch and blacked out Playa Girón completely. Three trucks with men from

the Milicias Nacionales Revolucionarias (MNR) were then observed moving toward the beach area without lights. These trucks discharged their troops, who moved in on the UDT team who were in position in some old ruins on the jetty. In total, there were 23 militia at Girón. The *Blagar* then moved in near the jetty to lend fire support to the landing. The Milicia troops were fired upon by the UDT team when they attempted to remove the red marker lights off the beach, followed shortly by the *Blagar*, clearing the beach completely in a few minutes. The only return fire was from one .50 calibre machine gun firing from the direction of the town, as shortly after, all the militia left the town and headed for Covadonga.

About 10 minutes later, the *Blagar* moved back and the first two LCVPs came in with men of the 4th Battalion from the *Caribe*. They struck the coral reef about 70 metres from the beach and tried to ride over it, but were unable to. They then dropped their ramps and the troops waded ashore.

Lynch's report continued:

The first troops came ashore yelling but once on the beach moved out quickly and quietly. The UDT team called the second two

LCVPs to land and warned them about the coral and had them come in slower and to discharge their troops as soon as they grounded on the coral. The brigade commander [Pérez San Román, together with his staff, including Ramon Ferrer, Raul de Varona and Manuel Artime, who would be the head of the exiles' government in Cuba] and his staff landed in a boat from *Blagar* at this time [01:15 a.m.; they used the small catamaran the ship was carrying] and took command of the beach. His radio was not working so his messages were relayed over the radio of the UDT team. There was no opposition to this landing as the fire from the *Blagar* had driven the militia away and no firing was heard until the troops started moving through the town..

As Lynch returned to the *Blagar* to direct the rest of the landing, and to prepare to go to Green Beach, the five men of the UDT team were left on the beach to find a landing site for the LCUs. They had the PRC-10 radio and the motor boat. The landing of troops continued and by first light all the 4th Battalion troops were ashore and the 6th Battalion was starting to land its troops ashore using the small boats from the *Río Escondido*. Two of the LCVPs were holed by coral, and after making several trips ashore, one (number 3) was forced to beach itself and the other sunk, but the crew was picked up and sent to the beach. This left the landing force with a much smaller landing capacity, making the landing slower than expected.

Commander Pérez San Román established his headquarters in a small building close to the landing beach, from where he would conduct the whole operation.

The UDT team continued to search for a landing site for the LCUs, with no luck, until a local fisherman was found and showed them a passage through the reef that could be used at high tide about 6:30 a.m. It was a narrow channel and could only be used by one LCU at a time. The channel was marked by buoys and at 6:00 a.m., the first LCU landed with one M-41, two REO trucks and one bulldozer. After this LCU was offloaded, it backed out and another moved into the channel. The empty one was sent to the *Río Escondido* to complete the offloading of the 6th Battalion. Around 7:30 a.m., all the vehicles and personnel of the two battalions had landed and the town of Girón was completely occupied, including the airfield.

Red Beach

Almost at the same time that the *Blagar* started the landing at Blue Beach, the *Barbara J.,* followed by the *Houston*, went to the end of the bay to land the 2nd and 5th Battalions at Red Beach, which was on Playa Larga, 39km to the north-west of Girón. According to Lynch:[30]

The UDT team from the *Barbara J.* led by Mr Robertson landed at about 01:30 and placed the marker light on the right side of the beach but was fired on from shore when attempting to place the left marker. This fire was from small automatic weapons and was silenced by the fire of the UDT team firing BARs and submachine [sic] guns from the rubber boat. The first troops of the 2nd Battalion started ashore in the small (19½ foot) boats of the *Houston* and the UDT team marked the left of the beach with a flashlight from 100 yards out in the rubber boat. The second wave received fire from shore while on the way in. This fire was silenced by the *Barbara J.* firing over the heads of the landing force. The militia fled leaving some of their weapons behind. Once ashore the troops moved through the town and cleaned it out. The landings continued until

all the 2nd Battalion minus one squad was ashore and the weapons company of the 5th Battalion landed also.

The troops on Red Beach were under the command of the second-in-command of the brigade, Erneido Oliva. At the small town of Playa Larga was a group of four men from the Navy's SV-3 patrol boat, with a dismounted .50 machine gun from the vessel, who were later joined by five men detached from Battalion 339 of the MNR. They were protecting the Buenaventura fishing co-operative, detached from its base at Cienfuegos to Central Australia sugar mill.

This group of soldiers saw the movement on the sea and, once they saw the ships approaching, opened fire against them with a machine gun.

When the first troops of 2nd Battalion arrived at the beach, they saw a truck full of militia and ordered them to surrender, but the militia opened fired instead, so the invaders fired back against the truck. Soldier Sergio Gilberto Díaz Morejón fired a bazooka against the truck, destroying it completely and killing 21 militia and 11 civilians. The militia forces on Playa Larga had been defeated, but not before their commander, Ramón González, alerted the command post at Central Australia. In the fight, one of the frogmen was killed, the first man of the brigade to die during the landing. According to Lynch:[31]

One survivor, the Company Commander of the weapons company of the 2nd Battalion stated that soon after daylight the beach was secured and they had captured over 40 prisoners. They discovered that 12 militia had been stationed in the town to guard a small militia radio station but that 30 or 40 had come in the day before on a picnic and were spending the night there.

As happened on Blue Beach, there were coral reefs that complicated the arrival of boats at the beach, while the outboard engines suffered numerous failures. This led to a delay in the landing, which began with the 2nd Battalion, and when dawn arrived, the 5th Battalion and most of the supplies were still on board the *Houston*. The arrival of the 5th Battalion was also delayed because its commander, Montero Duque, was no't convinced about landing as he claimed they did not had enough ammunition, he wasn't sure Castro had no artillery in the area and the landing boat engines were in a bad condition.

The troops of the 2nd Battalion advanced across the small town and occupied it, despite receiving fire from militia in the swamps on the other side of the road that went from there to Girón. After 15 minutes, the surviving militia escaped.

Airborne troops

On the afternoon of 16 April, the troops of the 1st Paratrooper Battalion, led by Alejandro del Valle, were briefed on their mission - Operation Halcón - for the next morning. They were to be dropped on the road from Central Australia to Playa Larga, and on a place called San Blas (14km from Girón), where the roads from Central Covadonga sugar mill (30km from Girón) and Yaguaramas (44km from Girón) merged to go to Girón. Five C-46s and one C-54 would take part in the mission, with two of the C-46s heading for the road from Playa Larga to Central Australia, each dropping 30 paratroopers, who were to attack the militias on Playa Larga from behind and prevent them receiving any support from Central Australia. The other planes were to drop the remaining 117 men on San Blas, to prevent troops coming from Yaguaramas and Central Covadonga from reaching Girón.

30 Grayston Lynch survey. National Defense University, Taylor Papers, Box 12, Cuba, Paramilitary Study. Secret; Eyes Only.

31 Grayston Lynch survey. National Defense University, Taylor Papers, Box 12, Cuba, Paramilitary Study. Secret; Eyes Only.

Landing boats used by the Brigade, both at Red and Blue beaches.

The planes had to be very precise in dropping the troops over the roads, as there were swamps on either side.

The planes took off at 2:20 a.m. (Nicaraguan time) and arrived over Bay of Pigs at 6:20 a.m. Cuban time, led by Eduardo Ferrer in the C-46 serialled 855. The force also comprised the C-46 serial 877 with pilot Navarro, 788 with Luaices, 878 with Tellechea and 864 with Gómez, and the C-54 serialled 7711 of Cereceda. They would also have the mission of making a reconnaissance of the airfield at Girón to see if it was usable by the B-26s and for sending in supplies.

When the planes arrived over Cuba, Ferrer saw the USS *Essex* and the escort destroyers, which gave his crew the confidence that there was no possibility of defeat. They approached the drop zone at 800ft and watched the landing unfolding on the bay.[32] Ferrer explains that 10 miles to the north of Girón he saw a jeep on the road whose occupants started to fire upon the planes. Once over the merged roads, Ferrer pushed the button to turn on the green light on, which was the order for the paratroopers to start jumping. Within 60 seconds all the troops were out of the plane, which made a turn to the east and returned to the drop zone to drop supplies for them. The returning planes flew in at 50ft and Ferrer made the reconnaissance of the runway at Girón. When they were over the sea, they saw a B-26; Ferrer initially thought it was one of theirs, but his co-pilot, Raúl Solís, shouted that it was a FAR plane and was opening fire on them. Ferrer turned towards the B-26 and the attacker had to pull down to avoid hitting the C-46. Immediately after, they headed to the ships, which opened fire on the B-26, forcing it to call off the chase.

Once on the ground, the paratroopers deployed themselves on the sides of the roads. Those dropped at San Blás divided, one group heading to Horquitas (36km from Girón), on the road to Yaguaramas, and the other to Jocuma, several kilometres towards Central Covadonga.

The battalion had platoons of 24 men, each platoon having a 7.62mm machine gun, bazooka, 60 mm mortar, 57mm recoilless gun and three BAR, with the rest armed with M-1 Garands, while those operating the machine guns and the Bazookas had M-3 sub-machine guns. They carried ten boxes of 2,500 7.62mm rounds, 12 mortar grenades, six bazooka rockets and eight rounds for the 57mm guns, while each paratrooper also carried 270 rounds of ammunition.[33]

As B Company was deployed over the town of Pálpite, between Playa Larga and Central Australia, one of the platoons of 27 men was dropped 2-3km from their target and only 2-3km from Central Australia. They stayed on a small hill and went to a farm, firing occasionally at enemy troops who were passing by the road from

Castro and Captain José Ramón Fernández at Central Australia.

Central Australia, killing Rebel Army Lieutenant Antero Fernández, commander of the troops based at Jagüey Grande.

The other platoon arrived near the small town of Pálpite, but did not enter it.

Castro's response

As soon as the militia on Playa Larga informed their command at Central Australia that the landing was taking place, they told La Habana, and at 3:29 a.m. Castro was informed of the situation. He asked for confirmation of the information, which arrived shortly after, adding that Playa Girón was also being occupied. Just before 4:00 a.m., they stop receiving news from Girón and Playa Larga, as the positions had fallen.

The first orders given by Castro were to blockade the exiles army's access to the Central Highway, which runs all across the island, as control of the highway would mean a fast advance towards La Habana. Batallón 339 of the Milicias Revolucionarias was the first unit moved, at 3:36 a.m., with orders to go from their deployment at Central Australia to Playa Larga (a distance of 28km) as quickly as they could. This unit had arrived at Central Australia between 8-10 April and comprised 528 men who had been fighting the counter-revolutionary guerrillas in the Escambray hills since the beginning of the year. Before their new deployment, their FAL rifles were changed for M-52s of inferior quality and shorter range. They also had BZ machine guns. Most of the men carried 90 rounds, while the machine gun operators carried 200 rounds.

The commander of the unit, Captain Ramón Cordero Reyes, sent two companies of his battalion on requisitioned vehicles, which

32 *Operación Puma*, Eduardo Ferrer, International Aviation Consultants, Inc. Florida, 1975.

33 *The Inevitable Battle, from the Bay of Pigs to Playa Girón*, Juan Carlos Rodríguez, Editorial Capitán San Luis, La Habana, Cuba, 2009.

Militia men received Czechoslovak sub-machine guns before being sent to the front at Bay of Pigs.

arrived near Playa Larga just before sunrise, but was easily beaten by the 2nd Battalion. The invaders were far better equipped and trained, and the militias suffered many casualties, the survivors dispersing after a short fight. In the meantime, the troops of E Company of the 2nd Battalion fired upon and destroyed a truck advancing towards them; however, the truck was being used by a group of civilians which were trying to flee the fighting, and at least four were killed. The remainder of Batallón 339 arrived after sunrise, headed by their commander, but they were also attacked from the rear by the paratroopers and forced to disengage. Captain Cordero Reyes managed to escape in a jeep to Central Australia, and, arriving around 9:00 a.m., said that his unit was either killed, wounded or dispersed. When asked which forces were left between the enemy and Central Australia, he replied: "There's nothing.". About 50 members of his unit managed to escape to Buenaventura and joined the crew of SV-3 patrol boat, then going to the town of Santo Tomás, 15km to the west. Others went to Soplillar, returned to Central Australia or made it to Los Alpes farm, near Jagüey Grande.

The troops of Batallón 2 took some prisoners from the defeated Cuban unit, who informed them that Castro was assembling his force in Central Australia to launch an attack.

A force comprising 300 men from Battalion 219 then arrived in Central Australia, followed by the Battalion 223 of the Milicias Revolucionarias, under the command of Captain Conrado Benítez, but none of them had any proper training (both units were still being organized at that time) and were armed with M-52 rifles with only 20 rounds each. They were sent to occupy the town of Pálpite, between Playa Larga and Central Australia, to avoid the enemy advancing towards the sugar mill (which was on the central highway). They marched to El Peaje, 8km south of Central Australia, where they were bombed by B-26s, suffering six fatalities and many wounded, forcing them to halt their advance.

They received orders to get in position there to face any advance towards Central Australia.

Several groups of men from Batallón 225, most of them from Jagüey Grande (a town near Central Australia) organized themselves and headed to the landing area without orders, getting into position around midday.

Around 9:30 a.m., the battalion-sized Escuela de Responsables de Milicias - a better-trained unit than the other Cuban forces in the area - arrived from Matanzas with 875 men and three doctors. They received orders to deploy at 3:30 a.m., and were told to occupy Pálpite; the second company of the unit would then advance to Soplillar, a small town 6km south-west of Pálpite and a few kilometres from the coast. The intention was, from there, to cut the road between Playa Larga and Girón. The town also had a small runway that they needed to keep out of the hands of the exiles.

By that time, the paratroopers near Pálpite had retreated to Playa Larga, largely because part of their supplies had fallen into the swamps. This made possible an easy occupation of the town by the Escuela de Responsables de Milicias at 12:37 p.m., and their second company headed as planned to Soplillar. The northern exit from the Ciénaga de Zapata was closed by Brigade 2506. After this unit's arrival, Batallón 227 of the Milicias was sent marching from Central Australia.

In the area of Playa Girón, Battalions 111 and 117 of the Milicias Revolucionarias, stationed at Las Villas and Cienfuegos respectively, received orders to move to Covadonga and Yaguaramas, and from there advance to San Blas. Late in the morning of the 17th, the incomplete Batallón 117 (with only two companies and an 85mm mortar company), under the command of Commander Filiberto Olivera Moya, reached the forward positions of the paratroopers at Horquitas and a fierce fight ensued, the airborne troops having received reinforcements from Girón, including one of the M-41 tanks. The invaders managed to hold their positions and the Batallón 117 returned to Yaguaramas. The other two companies of the battalion attacked from Covadonga to Jocuma.

Diversionary operations

The *Santa Ana* was sent with a small force of 168 men, headed by Higinio "Nino" Díaz, a former lieutenant of Movimiento 26 de Julio, escorted by two US destroyers, to land near Imías, in Oriente Province, about 70km from Guantánamo Base. The intention was to create a diversionary operation to distract Castro's troops to the area. They arrived to the area on the night of 13 April, discovering lights in the landing area, and assuming they were Cuban troops, it was suggested to delay the landing for 24 hours. A small boat landed at Mocambo beach, adjacent to Imías, commanded by Enrique Fernández Ruíz de la Torre. The militia saw the ships approaching on 14 April and were alerted to the attack; Díaz decided not to land when he spotted the movements of the militia on the coast. The ships sailed along the coast until 17 April, when they were requested to land at Bay of Pigs, but they arrived too late and returned to the United States.

The area around Santiago de Cuba and Guantanamo had recently been reinforced and was under the command of Commander Eddy Suñol. Three battalions were also placed at Baracoa, on the eastern end of the island, and others at Mangos de Baraguá, about 50km north of Santiago de Cuba, commanded byf Captain Senén Casas. The whoelarea was under the command of Commander Raúl Castro.

Another diversionary operation was mounted at Pinar del Río, on the western end of the island, with a ship equipped with electronic equipment to simulate that a landing was taking place there.

These two operations were successful in that they caused the Cuban command to send forces there, keeping these troops away from the operations around the Bay of Pigs.

CHAPTER 7
AIR COMBAT OVER BAY OF PIGS

The original plan for the Brigade's B-26s stated that a new air strike on the FAR air bases would take place at dawn on 17 April, with the aim of destroying the force's remaining combat planes, but this action was cancelled on the night of the 16th.

The plan for D-Day consisted of 11 primary targets to be attacked by 15 B-26 aircraft. Four of the primary targets - the three airfields which were struck on D-2 plus the Managua military base - were each to be attacked by two B-26s. Five other primary targets were double-headers, requiring single B-26 aircraft to hit two separate facilities. The remaining two targets were also to be attacked by single B-26s.

With the exception of the Managua military base - where napalm was to be employed against a big tank park seen on the U-2 photographs - all other targets were to be attacked with rockets, machine guns and either fragmentation or demolition bombs.[34]

According to the CIA:

The cancellation of the second strike - for on 16 April all of the targets, including restrikes at the D-2 airfields, were cancelled - turned a long planned, much discussed, tactical air operation into a 100 percent ground support mission for the invasion troops. By denying the requests from the field for a strike to eliminate (or at least reduce even further) Castro's fighters, it forced the Brigade B-26s into an unplanned and unwanted air combat role.[35]

Later, the list of targets was reduced to the air bases at San Antonio de los Baños and Ciudad Libertad and the naval bases at Batabano and Nueva Gerona, using only five planes, two to each base and one to attack the two naval facilities.

In the end, the air strikes against military facilities were cancelled, except for that against Nueva Gerona, where the patrol vessel *Baire* was anchored. It was also planned to fly operations over the beachhead, first of all bombing the forces approaching the landing area, while between 3:00 p.m. and 5:00 p.m. on 17 April, two B-26s would land at Playa Girón to start operating from there, without the use of extra fuel tanks, so they could receive the turrets for self-protection.

On the second day, they would perform exploration flights on the routes to the landing area and destroy any enemy force trying to approach the beachhead.

The sinking of the Baire
At 2:46 a.m. (Nicaraguan time), the first two B-26s took off from Happy Valley. They were the Linda 1, with Captain René García and Luis Ardois on plane 985, and Linda 2, with Captain Mario Cortina and Salvador Miralles on 930. They headed to the Isla de Pinos to attack the *Baire*, which it was feared could have gone to Bay of Pigs to intercept the landing vessels. According to García, the B-26s approached at 500ft and saw the *Baire* sailing to the east, outside the harbour, which was protected by AAA. Linda 1 started the attack, dropping its bombs, while Linda 2 made a pass with machine guns. They then made a second pass, firing their rockets, leaving the ship badly damaged and sinking. According to the commander of the *Baire*, Alférez de Fragata Gustavo Magnan, who was on board the

Castro's troops moving along Playa Larga while the Houston is still burning.

The *Baire*, which was sunk in the first air strike on 17 April.

vessel, they were not sailing, but anchored at Puerto Gerona, as they had one engine out of service and the other was in a bad condition. They opened fire with their 20mm machine guns and 3in gun, but they constantly jammed. Magnan said none of the bombs hit the vessel, but the planes' machine guns killed two men and wounded another two. The crew managed to start the only engine that was working and approached the pier of Nueva Gerona, where the ship sunk and turned on its side.

Supporting the beachhead
The two planes of Linda flight then headed to Bay of Pigs, where they met the Gorila flight, with Joaquín Varela and Tomás Afont on Gorila 1 (plane 945) and Gonzalo Herrera and Ángel López on Gorila 2 (929), who had taken off half an hour after the Linda planes. The four planes provided protection to the transports that were dropping the paratroopers, and then patrolled the area of Red Beach, being requested by the ground forces to attack the troops of Battalions 219 and 223. Linda 2 had expended all its ammunition in the attack on the *Baire*, so returned to Happy Valley, while the other three B-26s bombed the troops and destroyed many vehicles, as well as a small boat seen on the nearby Laguna del Tesoro (Treasure Lagoon).

At 3:45 a.m. (Nicaraguan time), Chico flight took off, with the plane serialled 935 with Captain Mario Zuñiga and Oscar Vega and 915 with Captain Matías Farías and Eddy González, heading for Blue Beach.

---

34 *Official history of the Bay of Pigs Operation*, Jack Pfeiffer, Central Intelligence Agency, 1979.

35 *Official history of the Bay of Pigs Operation*, Jack Pfeiffer, Central Intelligence Agency, 1979.

The FAR goes into action

At about 4:00 a.m., the pilots at San Antonio de los Baños were informed of the landing and that they had to prepare two Sea Furies, one T-33 and two B-26s, selecting Captain Carreras Rolas (commander of the Escuadrón de Persecución) and Lieutenant Bourzac to fly the Sea Furies, Lieutenant Alberto Fernández on the T-33 serialled 703 (which was put into service during the night) and Captain Silva Tablada and Lieutenant Álvaro Galo on the B-26s. Bourzac had little experience on the Sea Fury, having flown his first solo on the plane just a few days earlier and never fired any weapon with the plane, so this would be his first combat training.

The two Sea Furies were armed with two 250kg bombs and eight rockets, besides the 20mm guns. According to Carreras Rolas,[36] the Sea Furies were serialled 542 and 543, which means they had probably been changed prior to the invasion. He also stated that one of the B-26s, with Silva Tablada and gunners Adriano Sánchez and Pedro Delgado Lugo, was serialled 937. This B-26 had worn another serial and was dumped, but was recovered and put back into service some time earlier under the direction of the Chilean pilot Jack Lagas, who painted the Chilean flag and national motto "*Por la razón o por la fuerza*" on the nose.

At 5:40 a.m., the two Sea Furies and the B-26 of Silva Tablada took off and headed to Bay of Pigs. After 20 minutes they reached the bay and saw the whole landing unfolding below them. Carreras Rolas ordered Silva Tablada to attack the landing craft while he and Bourzac went to the *Houston*. Carreras dived at 60° and 700km/h, and the *Houston* and the *Barbara J.* immediately opened fire against him. He dropped his bombs but missed the target, then recovered and climbed to 1,500ft to make another attack, this time with the rockets, one of which hit the stern, causing severe damage to the *Houston*. Carreras made a third pass, firing his guns, wounding many on board before climbing to 7,000ft to return to base, ordering Bourzac to keep attacking the *Houston*, which he did, hitting the ship again with his rockets.

The captain of the *Houston*, Luis Morse, seeing he was sinking, beached the ship on the west side of the bay. Most of the 5th Battalion was still on board and had to land using the ship's life rafts, completing the landing around 5:00 p.m.. However, they landed in the swamps south-west of Playa Larga, having lost most of their equipment on the ship, and could not reach the combat zone. Erneido Oliva was authorized by San Román to relieve Duque as 5th Battalion commander and try to move the troops to Playa Larga, but when the unit had marched three miles they were stopped by a group of six Castro soldiers, the crew of SV-3 patrol boat and two others at Buenaventura, equipped with a 12.7mm machine gun, and Duque ordered them to turn back to where they had landed. When Duque was informed by Oliva that he was relieved of command, he turned off his radio and never told his troops. The unit dug trenches and remained there until the end of the action, when almost all of them were captured.

Immediately after, Fernández arrived at the Bay of Pigs with his T-33 and fired two rockets at an unknown vessel, most probably the *Barbara J.*, which was slightly damaged in one of the first air strikes. On a second pass, he fired the other two rockets at the same ship, continuing with a third pass when he fired his machine guns before returning to base.

While this was happening, Silva Tablada appeared from the east of Blue Beach and strafed the LCUs landing on the beach, causing damage to the motor of one LCVP, which proceeded onto the beach

Pilots posing with one of the Sea Furies before the invasion.

A pilot climbing on a FAR Sea Fury before a mission. The plane wears the colours used during the actions over Bay of Pigs.

Ground crews loading rockets on a Sea Fury of the FAR.

under its own power. There were no casualties from this attack and all anti-aircraft guns were firing on the B-26, which headed west in the direction of Red Beach. As the plane was leaving, two more aircraft were sighted coming from the west and they were opened fire on until it was discovered they were a friendly B-26 escorting a C-46 for the parachute drop. Silva Tablada's B-26 probably intercepted the C-46 of Eduardo Ferrer after his attack on the landing craft.

According to Grayston Lynch[37] in his report on the operation:

The blue wing bands that were to identify our planes could not be seen until the planes were overhead and proved to be of little value in telling friend from foe. The enemy air attacks, although practically continuous, were never in groups of over two planes

36 *Por el dominio del aire*, Enrique Carreras Rolas, Editora Política, La Habana 2008.

37 Grayston Lynch survey. National Defense University, Taylor Papers, Box 12, Cuba, Paramilitary Study. Secret; Eyes Only.

The T-33 FAR 703 at the time of the Bay of Pigs invasion.

A Sea Fury of the FAR armed with rockets.

FAR pilot Enrique Carreras Rolas with one of the Sea Furies of the FAR.

FAR pilot Rafael del Pino some years after the actions, in front of the FAR 711, one of the T-33s used at Bay of Pigs.

each. Each plane attacked independently and when he had fired his rockets left immediately. The only types observed were B-26s, which strafed and fired rockets, Sea Furys [sic] which usually only fired rockets (four) and T-33 jets which fired rockets also. The B-26s and Sea Furys [sic] were usually brought under AA fire with some effect but the T-33s always came from high out of the sun and we were never able to bring effective fire on them. After the first air attacks I called the brigade commander on the radio and advised him against moving the *Blagar* east to make the landing at Green Beach. The reasons given were that the departure of the *Blagar* would leave the ships in the beach area without their most effective anti-aircraft fire. Also by this time we had lost 3 of the 4 LCVPs and if the enemy planes hit us on our way down to Green Beach (a 2 hour trip), it might result in the loss of the battalion plus the command ship. I told him I could put the battalion ashore right away on Blue Beach by using the LCUs, and he could then start them toward Green Beach on the road. He agreed to this and two of the LCUs took this battalion ashore on Blue Beach.

Commander Pérez San Román then cancelled the landing at Green Beach and dropped the 3rd Battalion at Playa Girón, but with the order to head east and block any attempt by Castro's forces to approach from Cienfuegos.

Meanwhile, at San Antonio de los Baños, the order was given for the return of the Sea Fury and the B-26 that remained at Santiago de Cuba, while a new escadrille was prepared to fly to Bay of Pigs, including a Sea Fury that was put in service early that morning.

At 8:45 a.m., Captain Guillermo Figueroa took off on the T-33 serialled 711, with Silva Tablada and the Chilean pilot Jack Lagas on

two B-26s and Carreras, Bourzac and Nicaraguan pilot Carlos Ulloa on the Sea Furies.

Carreras first saw the *Houston* sinking and kept looking for other ships, when he spotted two B-26s of the Brigade diving upon him with machine guns blazing. They were probably the planes of Gorila flight, which were leaving the area, but Carreras started to climb, turning left, and dived at the bombers, firing his guns. The bombers headed towards the protection of the ships and Carreras disengaged, climbing to 7,000ft again, seeing the *Río Escondido* close to Blue Beach.

The two B-26s of Chico flight then arrived and Zuñiga went to intercept the Sea Fury of Carreras Rolas at the time the latter was diving to attack the *Río Escondido*. Carreras fired his rockets at the ship, hitting the deck, which was full of fuel drums which immediately caught fire. As he was diving, he felt the impact of the bullets fired by Zuñiga and the engine was damaged by a bullet in one cylinder, but he managed to return to base.

Zuñiga then attacked the plane of Bourzac, who was attacking the *Houston* again, and according to Eduardo Ferrer,[38] they entered in an air combat, performing a scissors manoeuvre; when Bourzac attempted to make a fast climb to descend and attack the B-26, Zuñiga fired two rockets at him but missed. Bourzac disengaged and returned to base. Farías tried unsuccessfully to intercept him and then to intercept the plane of Carreras, who was flying slowly due to the damage to his engine. Farías fired on the Sea Fury and claimed he hit the plane on the engine too,[39] despite Carreras only recalling being hit while attacking the *Río Escondido*.[40] Farías then returned to Bay of Pigs and stayed over the area, attacking troops that were approaching from Cienfuegos and the militia units at Soplillar and Yaguaramas, which were fighting with the paratroopers.

Zuñiga, with his plane damaged because of high Gs (due to vertical acceleration during manoeuvres), pulled out of the combat area and had to return to Grand Cayman, waiting to be evacuated on the following day by a C-54.

Carlos Ulloa in his Sea Fury went to attack the landing vessels and strafed the damaged *Río Escondido*, but he was hit by machine guns from the *Blagar*, shot down and killed. The *Río Escondido* was abandoned by her crew, who were rescued by the landing vessels, and a few minutes later exploded and sank.

In the meantime, Captain Guillermo Figueroa returned to base without firing his weapons and was arrested, while Jack Lagas (flying the plane with serial 937) attacked an unidentified ship with machine guns on his first pass. Then he attacked the landing craft, and finally he saw a B-26 and went to intercept it, claiming he damaged it. This was most probably the plane of Farías, who stated seeing a FAR B-26 with which he exchanged fire without hits on either side. Lagas ran out of ammunition and then returned to base feeling very depressed and scared by his combat mission, and according to Del Pino, never flew again during the operations, despite Carreras and others stating that he flew another mission that day, two missions on 18 April and three the following day.

Farías realized he hadn't enough fuel to return to Happy Valley, and planned to divert to Grand Cayman or Jamaica, but when he saw the landing strip at Girón decided to land there. Then he was attacked by an unknown Sea Fury, which left the interception shortly after.

At around 10:35 a.m., the T-33 of Alberto Fernández and the B-26 of Álvaro Galo (who was from Nicaragua) appeared over Bay of Pigs. Galo, seeing the fierce AAA and not willing to risk his life, flew over the area and returned to base without dropping his bombs, and was consequently arrested.

Fernández, seeing the plane of Matías Farías to the north of Playa Larga, intercepted him, damaging the plane extensively and killing navigator Eddy González with a shot in the head. Farías decided to attempt to land at Girón airfield, but when he was about to land he was hit again by Fernández and crashed, being thrown out of the plane and severely wounded. However, he was rescued by the brigade's ground forces and survived.

38 *Operación Puma*, Eduardo Ferrer, International Aviation Consultants, Inc. Florida, 1975.
39 *Foreign Invaders*, Dan Hagedorn and Leif Hellström, Midland Publishing, Leicester, 1994.
40 *Por el dominio del aire*, Enrique Carreras Rolas, Editora Política, La Habana 2008.

An unmarked Sea Fury of the FAR before the Bay of Pigs actions.

A Sea Fury of the FAR armed with rockets.

One of FAL's B-26s painted with nose art before the actions. It was removed before the first strikes.

According to Grayston Lynch, at that time,

[A] message was sent to Headquarters advising them of the loss of the two ships and an answer was received directing us to take all the rest of the ships to sea and return and unload under the cover of darkness. At this time we were attacked by a B-26 [probably Galo's plane] and the fire from the ships and from a friendly B-26 sent him away smoking. The *Barbara J.* and the two cargo ships, the *Caribe* and the *Atlántico* were told to proceed ahead of us and wait 15 miles out. At this time I called the UDT team of 5 men ashore on Blue Beach and told them to return to the ship as we were going out to sea and return that night. They replied that they would stay on the beach and light it for us when we returned that night. All these men

One of the FAR's Sea Furies before the invasion.

The *Houston* burning near Playa Larga.

The remains of Matías Farías' B-26 at Girón Airfield.

The wreckage of the B-26 of Matías Farías, shot down on 17 April while he was attempting to land at Girón Airfield.

were captured when Blue Beach fell. The *Blagar* was to escort the three LCUs which could only do six knots.[41]

The FAR dominates the beachhead

At mid-morning, Captain Álvaro Prendes departed on the T-33 serialled 711 to attack the ships that were leaving Bay of Pigs, approaching the landing area at very low altitude with the intention of remaining unseen. He then started to fly over the sea, saw the ships sailing to the south-east, aimed at what he identified as a landing vessel and fired his four rockets. He had caught the gunners by surprise and

41 Grayston Lynch survey. National Defense University, Taylor Papers, Box 12, Cuba, Paramilitary Study. Secret; Eyes Only.

the AAA was light. Prendes climbed, turning left, and prepared for another pass, this time using his two machine guns. He fired at the ship despite there now being very heavy AAA, and escaped, seeing the tracers passing close to his plane. He then felt an impact, but everything appeared normal. The ship was probably the *Barbara J.*, which informed the *Blagar* that it had been damaged by rockets and was leaving the bay towards Blue Beach. Prendes then turned towards San Antonio de los Baños, but when he landed, the plane swerved uncontrollably to the right and ended up off the runway, but undamaged. The mechanics found that a shot had blocked the right wheel brake. The T-33 was swiftly repaired and was ready to fly again that afternoon.

In the meantime, the two B-26s of Lobo flight from Puerto Cabezas arrived over the area of operations, having departed at 6:40 a.m. (Nicaraguan time). One of the planes was flown by Gustavo Ponzoa and Rafael García Pujol, with that serialled 928 by Ignacio Rojas and Esteban Bovo Carás. Rojas attempted to eject the extra fuel tanks, but one remained hanging below the wing and Ponzoa ordered him to return to base. Ponzoa then made contact with the *Houston*, which requested air cover over the ships. The B-26 remained on patrol for a while, then, when he was almost ready to return due to low fuel, Ponzoa saw a T-33 climbing towards them and passing about 500 metres ahead, without seeing their bomber. Ponzoa fired on the T-33 without hitting it (it was probably Prendes' plane), and almost at the same time the planes of Paloma flight arrived, so he headed back to Puerto Cabezas. On his return, he saw the planes of León flight over the sea.

At San Antonio de los Baños, another mission was prepared, comprising a B-26 with Silva Tablada, a Sea Fury with Bourzac and the T-33 serialled 703 with Rafael del Pino. According to Del Pino, he was armed with the last rockets they had for the T-33s. Silva Tablada was carrying five 250kg bombs and his 12.7mm machine guns, and had Jesús Noa Díaz as navigator and Sergeants Reinaldo González Galainena and Martín Torres Ruiz as gunners. The two prop planes would make the first strikes, with Del Pino acting as air cover at 3,000ft, and once they had finished he would descend to make his attack.

At the same time, the two B-26s of Paloma flight, with Captain Osvaldo "Chirrino" Piedra and Joe Fernández in the lead and the 927 with Captain Antonio Soto and Benito González, appeared over Bay of Pigs. They were seen by Del Pino, who, approaching the area, saw a B-26 heading at 180°. He asked Silva Tablada if he had changed course, but he answered he was keeping his course to the ships, with heading 130°. He descended from 7,000ft, and at 800 metres saw the blue stripes that indicated it was a plane of the invaders. Del Pino applied the air brakes and approached the B-26 until he was very close, then opened fire. He then felt an impact on his plane and thought he was hit, but it was a piece of the B-26 that had been hit and fallen off.

The B-26 was that commanded by "Chirrino" Piedra, which crashed and both crew members were killed. This action was seen by the two A-4Bs, commanded by Jim Forgy and Tim Lanaham, which were at 25,000ft over international waters, unable to intervene.

Del Pino immediately called Silva Tablada and asked for his position, receiving a reply that he was 10 miles to the south of Cienfuegos with two ships in sight at 15 miles. Silva started the attack, diving with Bourzac behind him. The AAA from the ships opened fire and Silva did the same with his machine guns, despite being out of range. Before he could reach the ships, their artillery hit him and he lost his left wing, falling immediately into the sea, with some pieces bouncing and passing over the *Blagar*.

The other plane of Paloma flight went to attack the enemy troops on the beachhead, and suffered damage to one engine from the AAA, having to return to Grand Cayman, where it made an emergency landing.

Bourzac continued his attack against the ship that was at the end of the line of vessels, at the same time that Del Pino approached to fire his rockets, which he did at about 300 metres from the ship - which had to divide its fire between the two planes - and claimed a hit on the ship with one of them.

According to Grayston Lynch:

When we reached the 15 mile point we called the other ships and told them to assemble on us but only the *Barbara J.* showed up. The two cargo ships could not be found nor would they answer the radio calls. Soon after the *Barbara J.* rejoined us we were attacked by a B-26 and a Sea Fury coming from the beach area. The B-26 started an approach on the *Blagar* but was hit and as the plane fired its rockets it exploded in flames. The rockets struck 50 yards from the *Blagar* and the plane hit the water in the same place and bounced over the ship clearing the deck by only 20 feet. It struck the water about 100 yards over the ship and burned and sank. Parts of the plane were scattered over the deck of the *Blagar*. The Sea Fury did not press his attack but made one short strafing pass at the *Barbara J.* hitting her with two or three 20 mm shells. He then threw four rockets at the LCUs from a high altitude all of which missed and he departed. Two more attacks were made on us later in the day by lone B-26s none of which pressed the attack. The AAA fire held them at a distance and they fired their rockets wide of the targets.[42]

Shortly after Del Pino and Bourzac landed at San Antonio de los Baños, Douglas Rudd arrived from Santiago de Cuba with a Sea Fury, which was immediately prepared for action over the combat zone.

Álvaro Prendes took off with the T-33 711 as soon as the plane was repaired, an hour after returning from his previous mission, and approached Bay of Pigs flying at over 10,000ft, searching for the enemy B-26s, as they were informed the ships were leaving the area.

Meanwhile, León flight was approaching from Puerto Cabezas, with the 907 with Captain Crispín García and Juan M. González. The leader of the flight, the 923 with Captain Miguel Carro Suárez and Eduardo Barea Guinea, had to abort due to a failure after take-off, so Crispín García was flying alone. He stayed over the beachhead, providing close air support until, after an air strike close to Soplillar, he was seen by Prendes at the moment he was climbing after dropping his ordnance. Prendes reduced power, used his air brakes and began his attack, but García saw him and headed for some clouds as fast as he could. Prendes opened fire with his two machine guns, knowing that he would only have one chance before the B-26 entered the clouds, and hit the plane in its left engine and wing. García made a turn and entered the clouds, flying north. He finally managed to land at Boca Chica.

On the night of 17 April, García and González were ordered to fly to Puerto Cabezas with the plane serialled 933 that had landed there two days earlier, as this plane was still operational. They departed but never arrived in Nicaragua, the wreckage of the plane and their bodies being found in November 1961 in the woods of Jinotega Department in Nicaragua.

Last air combat of the day

After attacking García's plane, Prendes returned to base and received orders to take off at 2:00 p.m. with the T-33 serialled 709, with Rafael del Pino on the T-33 711 and Douglas Rudd in a Sea Fury to look for more enemy planes.

While this was happening, Puma flight was approaching the beachhead and, according to Ferrer,[43] was over Bay of Pigs around 3:05 p.m. The escadrille was formed by the plane of Captain José Alberto Crespo and Lorenzo Pérez Lorenzo and the 935 plane with Captain Raúl Viannello and Demetrio Pérez. They made contact with the commander at Red Beach, Erneido Oliva, who sent them to attack a convoy of troops of the Escuela de Responsables de Milicias approaching Playa Larga from Central Australia. They made three passes, dropping their bombs, firing rockets and strafing, causing many casualties and destroying vehicles. As the lead Puma expended all its ammunition, the second plane spotted a machine gun position near Central Australia and went to attack it, while the former awaited its return.

As the ships couldn't unload all their cargo, Eduardo Ferrer was asked to go with a C-46 to land at Playa Girón airfield and leave a load of ammunition, escorted by a single B-26 armed only with machine guns and crewed by Captain Miguel Carro Suárez and Eduardo Barea Guinea (whose plane was repaired after they aborted the previous mission). Ferrer decided to take off at 2:00 p.m. to arrive at sunset. Priest Cavero, who was with the brigade at the base, asked to go with them. Despite Ferrer's refusal, he convinced him and was accepted to go, armed with a Browning Automatic Rifle M1918, while crewman Alberto Pérez, who managed the cargo, was carrying another Browning: the intention was to use them against any fighter that attempted to attack the transport, to at least spoil its aim.

With callsign Elefante 1, they took off overloaded, using the entire

42 Grayston Lynch survey. National Defense University, Taylor Papers, Box 12, Cuba, Paramilitary Study. Secret; Eyes Only.

43 *Operación Puma*, Eduardo Ferrer, International Aviation Consultants, Inc. Florida, 1975.

The remains of the FAR 935 of Matías Farías at Girón Airfield.

Enrique Carreras Rolas in front of his T-33, while mechanics prepare the plane for another mission. The plane, with serial 703, was put in service during the actions of April.

A FAR B-26C wearing special camouflage received at the time of the Bay of Pigs invasion. It is not clear if the camouflage was received before or after the actions. Several Invaders still wore the old silver colours during the actions.

Three abandonded LCVPs lie near the beaches of Girón, after being lost when the coral reefs damaged their hulls.

runway of Puerto Cabezas, and headed to Playa Girón, with the B-26 (callsign Elefante 2) taking off later, as it was much faster than the C-46, which could only reach 120 knots with the load it was carrying. At 4:00 p.m., Carro Suárez informed them their extra fuel tanks were not transferring, but that he would land at Playa Girón with the C-46 to refuel, or at Grand Cayman on the return. Twenty minutes later they tested the machine guns, finding they were jammed, but they decided to keep escorting the transport until they were ordered by Ferrer and Captain Crispín García, who was departing the area, to return. Carro Suárez then turned back and headed to Happy Valley, leaving the C-46 alone.

At that moment, Prendes, in his T-33, was informed by headquarters at Central Australia of the attack of the B-26s of Puma flight and the three planes headed there, descending. They saw the planes ahead (Prendes says Del Pino saw them first[44] and Del Pino states it was Prendes who saw them first[45]), and Prendes went for the plane that was closer and ordered Del Pino and Rudd to go for the other.

Prendes attacked the plane of Viannello head-on, forgetting the B-26 was armed with eight machine guns on the nose. Both planes opened fire at the same time and Prendes was forced to turn fast to the left to avoid the fire from the B-26. He kept turning left as hard as

he could and saw the B-26 approaching the coast, and when Viannello saw the T-33 approaching from behind, he started to turn as tight as possible, as the turning radius of the B-26 was smaller than that of the T-33. The first burst of machine guns by Prendes failed and when he attempted to fire for a second time, the B-26 turned hard to the left, leaving Prendes to his right, so he opened the air brakes to reduce speed. The B-26 headed fast over the sea, but then Prendes managed to approach at a 250° angle and opened fire, hitting the B-26 in the side, from nose to tail. He passed very close to the plane and climbed, seeing the B-26 was still flying low and fast over the sea, heading to Puerto Cabezas. Prendes made another pass, firing with his two machine guns and hitting the fuselage, turning for another attack, this time as slow as possible, to keep the enemy plane in his sights for as long as he could. He approached from behind and fired until extremely close to the B-26, seeing parts falling from the plane and black smoke pouring from the left engine. Prendes started to climb to return to base while he kept watching the B-26, whose left engine caught fire. He said he saw a crew member jumping from the plane just a few seconds before it hit the water and exploded. Viannello had headed towards the US destroyers to look for protection and to be recovered, as he realized he couldn't reach his base. He ordered Pérez to jump when they were close to the ships, which he did from a height of 1,000ft and was rescued by the USS *Murray*, but Viannello then crashed with the plane and was killed.

As the C-46 of Ferrer approached Playa Girón airfield, he realized he was being escorted by two A-4B Skyhawks from the USS *Essex* aircraft carrier, without any markings, which were sent to cover the Brigade's planes but with orders only to put themselves between FAR planes and Brigade ones, being authorized only to fire if they were fired upon.

44 *En el punto rojo de mi kolimador. Crónicas de un aviador.* Álvaro Prendes, Editorial Letras Cubanas, La Habana, 1982.

45 *9050 Horas*, Rafael del Pino, Miami, 2012.

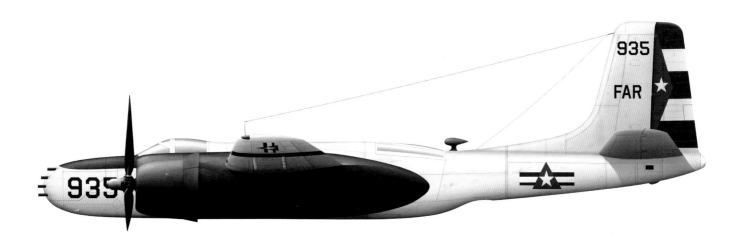

Douglas B-26B Invader used by the Fuerza Aérea de Liberación, wearing the FAR colours
but with blue stripes on the wings for identification. (Luca Canossa)

The Douglas A-4B Skyhawks on USS Essex received grey paint over all their markings, in an attempt to avoid
identification, despite the FAR pilots who saw them never doubted they were US planes. (Luca Canossa)

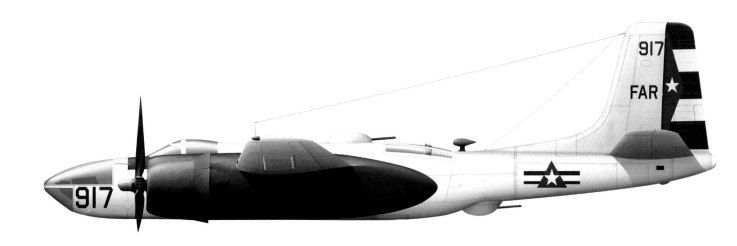

A Douglas B-26C Invader of the FAR. Among the differences with the exiles' planes, they had two turrets, a glass nose and didn't wear blue stripes. (Luca Canossa)

One of the Curtiss C-46 Commando planes used by the Fuerza Aérea de Liberación for transport and to drop the paratroopers over the Zapata swamps. (Luca Canossa)

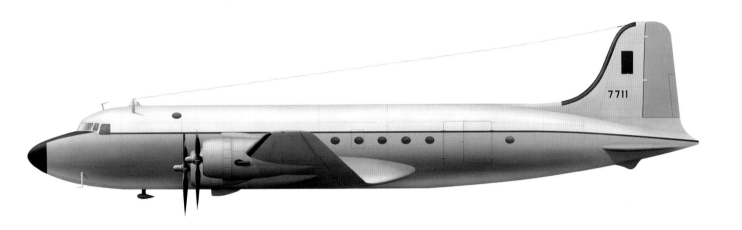

One of the Douglas C-54 provided by the CIA to the exiles' air force. (Luca Canossa)

A Republic P-47D Thunderbolt of the Fuerza Aérea del Ejército de Cuba, as was the name of the Cuban Air Force before the revolution. The P-47s were not operational by the time of the Bay of Pigs invasion, but some were used as decoys. (Luca Canossa)

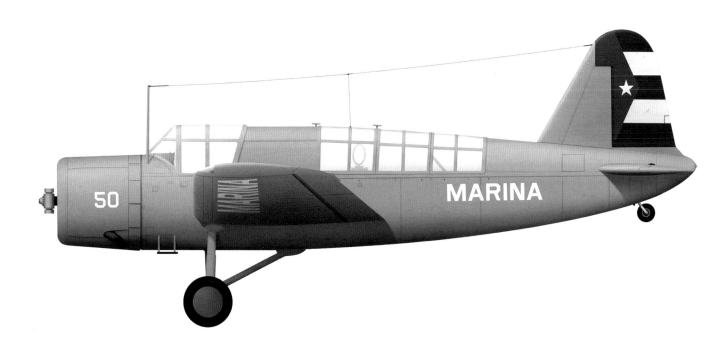

This Vought Kingfisher was one of the first plane used by the Movimiento 26 de Julio, when its pilot made a forced landing on a rebel controlled airfield and was captured. Now it's preserved at the Museo de la Revolución. (Luca Canossa)

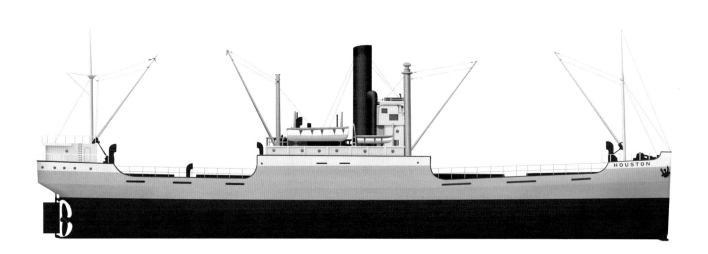

The *Houston* was one of the García Line's merchant ships leased for the operations and sunk near Playa Larga, when she was disembarking the Batallón 5. (Luca Canossa)

A REO M35 truck armed with a Browning M2 12.7 mm machine gun as used by the Brigade 2506. (Luca Canossa)

One of the Hawker Sea Furies used by the FAR during the Bay of Pigs actions. They were the most powerful fighters of the force by then, but poor maintenance led to them having many technical problems. Also, one was shot down. (Luca Canossa)

Another Sea Fury as used during the Bay of Pigs. The plane were wearing different camouflage patterns, as they were painted with what was available. (Luca Canossa)

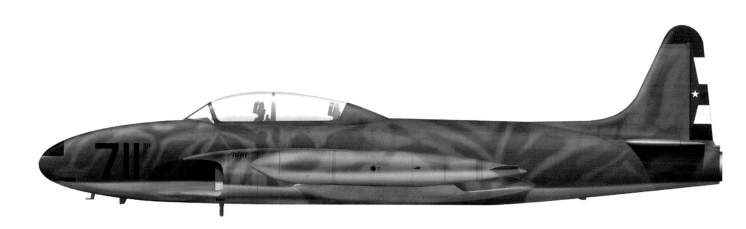

The Lockheed T-33s were camouflaged shortly before the invasion, when the Cuban government realized that an invasion was imminent. Despite their light fire power, they were very effective against the defenceless B-26s of the exiles. (Luca Canossa)

An M41 medium tank as used by the Brigade 2506, they were very successful on the battle at Playa Larga, against the T-34s. Training of the crews was essential, together with a good planning of the defence positions, to win the night battle. (Luca Canossa)

The Cuban T-34 tanks were sent into battle, but the poor training of the crews, which received the new tanks shortly before the actions, led to a very poor performance of them in the battle, with many being destroyed by the M41s and the bazookas. (Luca Canossa)

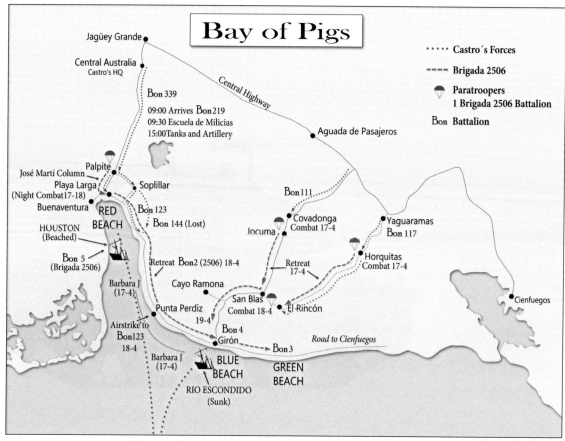

Map of the Bay of Pigs with the main actions from both sides. (Luca Canossa)

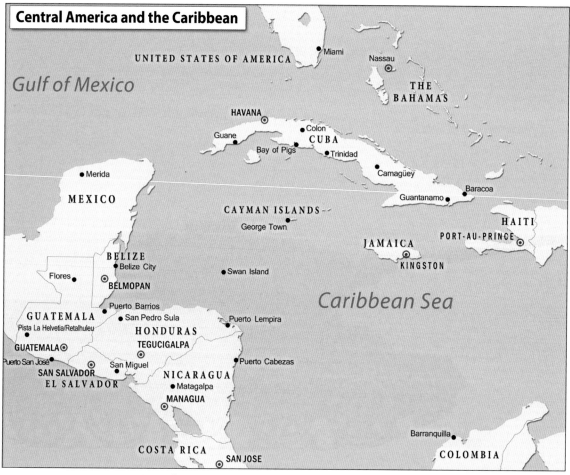

Map of Central America and the Caribbean. (Luca Canossa)

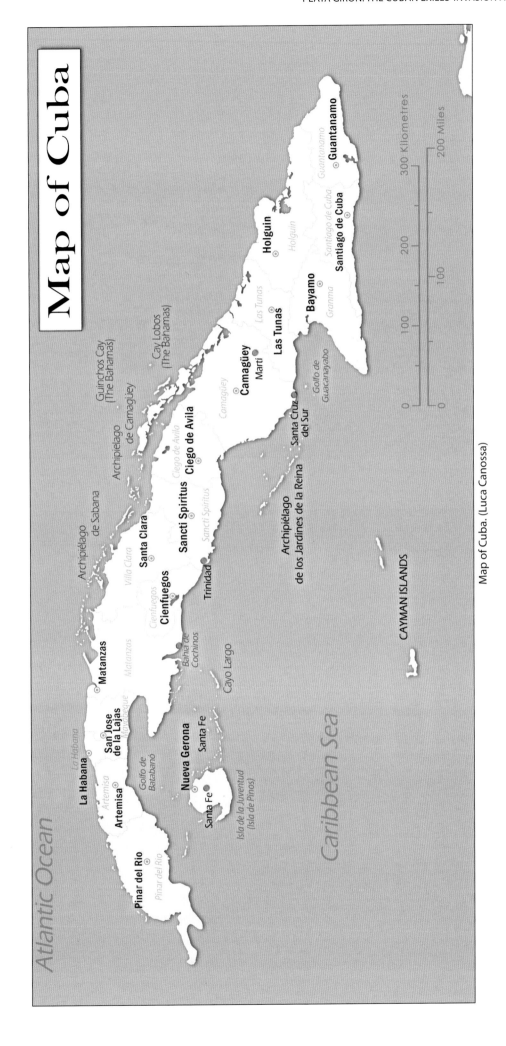

Map of Cuba

Map of Cuba. (Luca Canossa)

The FAR serialled 703 was one of the T-33s used at Bay of Pigs and preserved at the FAR museum. (Photo: Andres Hernandez Reyes)

One of the Sea Furies preserved at the Museo de la Revolución in La Habana. (Photo: Amaru Tincopa)

A Sea Fury preserved at Playa Girón Museum.

A tractor modified with armour during the revolution and used at the front headed by Camilo
Cienfuegos in the zone of Las Villas province, to the west of the country.

A boat used by Brigada 2506 during ther landing, preserved at the Museo de la Revolución in La Habana.

A captured M-41 tank of Brigada 2506 at Playa Girón Museum.

A P-51D Mustang purchased by the rebels in late 1959 but not used in combat, serialled FAR-401, which was preserved by the FAR. (Photo: Craig Walker)

An SU-100 self propelled gun preserved at Playa Girón Museum.

A T-34 tank preserved at Playa Girón Museum.

An SU-100 preserved at La Habana.

An M-43 120mm heavy mortar preserved at Playa Girón Museum.

An M53 anti-aircraft gun, called "Cuatro Bocas" in Cuba, preserved at Playa Girón Museum.

The T-33 FAEC-703 seen before 1959. The plane is currently preserved.

The B-26B with serial 931 preserved at Miami, currently as a monument for Brigada 2506.

The badge of the paratroopers of Brigada 2506.

The badge of Brigada 2506.

Two of the crew members and the priest, in the cargo cabin of the C-46, opened fire against the fighters from the emergency windows of the plane, thinking they were from the FAR. Ferrer ordered them to cease firing, not because they could damage the A-4s but because they could damage their own C-46. Shortly after, the Skyhawks left them.

While Prendes was intercepting the plane of Viannello, Del Pino and Rudd went for the other B-26, commanded by Crespo, which was descending as fast as it could to fly very low over the sea. Del Pino placed the bomber in his sights and opened fire while diving. Rudd alerted him of the altitude and he levelled out at about 20 metres over the sea. After levelling, he lost the B-26, but it was caught by Rudd, who damaged its left engine. When he was preparing his Sea Fury to make another attack, the two Skyhawks - one of them commanded by Jim Forgy - appeared and placed themselves between Rudd and the B-26 of Crespo, forcing Rudd to leave the action as he couldn't fire without hitting the Skyhawks. Despite the pilots of the Skyhawks requesting permission to shoot down Rudd, this was denied.

According to Eduardo Ferrer, the B-26 of Crespo kept flying but was losing fuel fast, with the left engine in trouble. Ferrero decided to return without landing and trying to escort the B-26, which they couldn't see. They kept communicating with the C-46 and said they were heading to Puerto Cabezas, but an hour before arriving they made their last communication, saying they were going to ditch the plane, something almost impossible in a B-26 and even more so at night. Nothing more was heard nor found of them.[46]

Del Pino then went to attack the enemy positions at Playa Larga to spend his ammunition, and both planes returned to base. This was the last mission of the day and left a very successful balance to the FAR, while to the Brigade's air arm (the Fuerza Aérea de Liberación) it demonstrated that with FAR fighters still operational, it wasn't possible to provide support to ground forces nor the ships, as the B-26s, without their defensive turrets, were extremely vulnerable to the fighters.

At the end of the day, the Fuerza Aérea de Liberación had less than half of the original 16 to 18 planes of its fleet, as four were shot down, one disappeared and crashed in Nicaragua, one was damaged at Boca

46 *Operación Puma*, Eduardo Ferrer, International Aviation Consultants, Inc. Florida, 1975.

Álvaro Prendes with the T-33 serialled 711 after the actions. The plane wears the last camouflage used by the planes.

Chica, the defecting one was at Miami and three had landed at Grand Cayman and remained there. To increase the fleet, four additional B-26s were sent to Puerto Cabezas from the United States late on 18 April, with extra fuel tanks installed inside. Some of the planes at Grand Cayman were recovered to Puerto Cabezas during 18 and 19 April, but it is unclear if all were recovered before the invasion was over.

In an attempt to destroy more FAR planes on the ground, a mission with four planes was ordered for the night of 17 April to bomb San Antonio de los Baños Air Base. The plane serialled 985 would fly with Captain Joaquín Varela and Tomás Afont, escorted by another plane with Captain Ignacio Rojas and Esteban Bovo Carás, while the plane serialled 923 with Captain Gonzálo Herrera and Ángel López would be escorted by the 927 of Captain Mario Cortina and Salvador Miralles. They arrived over the base, but it was in darkness, as were the surrounding towns, and the AAA also did not open fire to avoid showing their positions. Varela fired his rockets and dropped his bombs, trying to attract the AAA and then identify the base position, but nothing happened. The planes therefore returned to base without success. Varela's ordnance actually fell close to the base, but caused no damage.

CHAPTER 8:
THE GROUND BATTLE IN THE AFTERNOON AND NIGHT

Playa Larga
As soon as the Escuela de Responsables de Milicias reached Pálpite, they were bombed by the B-26s, with 22 men killed and many wounded. Their situation and the strong position of Batallón 2 of Brigada 2506 at Playa Larga forced them to stay at Pálpite in a defensive position, waiting for reinforcements to launch an attack against the invaders. During the rest of the day, until sunset, only small skirmishes took place on the road connecting the two towns.

Batallón 5 was lost, as they landed in the swamps to the west of Bay of Pigs when the *Houston* was sunk and were more than 10km from Playa Larga, with no roads to help reach the town. Erneido Oliva managed to talk with San Román and asked for reinforcements, receiving, at 2:00 p.m., two M-41 tanks, two trucks with ammunition, one recoilless gun and some infantry from Batallón 4 and Batallón 6. With these reinforcements, they had about 370 men.

According to Grayston Lynch,[47] an attack by the Escuela de Responsables de Milicias[48] was launched against Playa Larga after the reinforcements arrived, being spotted at 2:30 p.m. advancing towards the town and halting very close to the positions of Batallón 2 at 2:45 p.m. without noticing the presence of the enemy. Lynch continued:

This attack was launched down the road from the north. The troops, all militia, were in open, 2.5 ton trucks and open, semi-trailer trucks. The fire of the tanks and the 57 recoil-less [sic] guns, 3.5s and the 12.7mm caliber machine guns of the landing force hit them

47 Grayston Lynch survey. National Defense University, Taylor Papers, Box 12, Cuba, Paramilitary Study. Secret; Eyes Only.

48 The same author, in his book *Decision for Disaster*, states that this unit was Batallón 339, but most Cuban sources indicate that unit was defeated at 9:00 a.m.

The first T-34 tank destroyed during the night combat at Playa Larga. To the left, an M-35 truck abandoned by the Brigade can be seen.

A T-34 tank destroyed during the night battle lies on the side of a road near Playa Larga.

One of the M-41 tanks used by the Brigade. In the fight at Playa Larga, they were one of the key elements in the victory of the Brigade.

before they could get out of the trucks. This force was estimated at 1,500 and all the survivors of this action claimed they killed or wounded over half of them and destroyed most of the trucks.

In fact, casualties from this combat were far fewer less and the unit regrouped after retreating.

Shortly after, the vanguard of Batallón 2 spotted two ambulances and a Red Cross truck approaching and stopping near the wounded and dead of the enemy unit, but instead of recovering the enemy, they started to deploy mortars and were followed by trucks with troops. The order was given to open fire upon them, destroying the vehicles and forcing the enemy to retreat.

After this combat, Batallón 2 forces started to repair the trucks that had survived the blasting of the UDT team during the landing. Later on, they were informed that another M-41, the remainder of Batallón

4 and a company of Batallón 6 would be sent as reinforcements, as Oliva learned from prisoners that a large force was being assembled at Central Australia to attack during the night. These fresh invading troops arrived around 6:00 p.m. One of the trucks carrying reinforcements flipped over on the road to Playa Larga, and they stayed the night there until they were recovered the next day at midday when the forces from Playa Larga retreated.

Meanwhile, Fidel Castro moved his headquarters to Central Australia to direct the troops from the field, arriving at 3:00 p.m. to meet General José Ramón Fernandez, who was in charge of the headquarters until then. Shortly after, four batteries with a total of twenty-four 122mm howitzers arrived from Matanzas under command of Lieutenant Roberto Milián Vega, plus a battery of six 85mm guns and one of six 120mm mortars. Also with Castro were six batteries of Czech 12.7mm M-53 quadruple anti-aircraft machine guns - the "Cuatro Bocas" (Four Mouths) - a battery of 37mm anti-aircraft guns and five T-34 tanks command by Lieutenant Néstor López Cuba. The anti-aircraft weapons were deployed around Central Australia to protect the area from the B-26s, while the artillery and tanks were prepared to attack the enemy positions at Playa Larga that night, when the infantry would try to take the town. Castro's intention was to destroy the brigade during the night and recover all the territory by sunrise.

To prepare this attack, at 5:00 p.m., Castro moved his headquarters to Pálpite. He would use the troops of the Columna 1 Especial de Combate José Martí, who were veterans of the Rebel Army with experience from the revolution, under command of Harold Ferrer Martínez. This unit was formed of four infantry companies, one company of mortar batteries, a machine-gun company and a small force of flamethrowers, plus two companies with Super Bazookas that were already deployed there and were subordinated to the column. In total, they numbered around 600 men. They were to attack together with the tanks, and with support from the artillery and the Escuela de Responsables de Milicias.

Batallón 144 of the militia received orders to go to Soplillar and from there to cut the road between Playa Larga and Playa Girón, but they get lost during the night and never reached the road before the Brigade 2506 forces at Red Beach retreated to Playa Girón on 18 April. They were then shelled by their own artillery, which thought they were part of the Brigade's forces, and were also bombed by enemy planes.

General José Ramón Fernández ordered the 85mm guns to open fire sporadically, with further fire from the 120mm mortars, located 4km from the enemy. The mortar fire was ineffective as the first shots were fired without fuses and the shells didn't explode.

The night battle

Before launching the attack on Playa Larga, Castro received information that another landing was taking place to the west of La Habana and decided to return to the capital instead of leading the attack, as he had planned. When he reached La Habana, at sunrise, he was informed that no landing had taken place (this was the deception operation mounted by the CIA to the west of the island) and returned to Bay of Pigs, but too late to take part in the combat at Playa Larga.

At midnight on 18 April, 1 and 3 companies of the Escuela de Responsables de Milicias (with about 300 men) and the rocket launcher company began the approach to Playa Larga, following the road, with Columna 1 Especial de Combate behind, together with five T-34 tanks. As they could only advance on the 25-metre wide road, they could not deploy, being forced to march in lines.

Meanwhile, the 122mm guns of Castro's forces had opened fire against the beach at 7:30 p.m., initially with very poor efficiency, with

Cuban field artillery firing against the positions of the Brigade.

A 122mm howitzer of the Cuban Rebel Army firing against the positions of the Brigade.

Cuban militia firing a Soviet M30 122mm howitzer against enemy positions.

Rebel Army troops and militia firing M30 122mm howitzers against the Brigade.

Militia marching to Bay of Pigs armed with Czechoslovak Vz-52 rifles.

their shells falling close to the positions of the 81mm mortars, but then they started landing to the south until falling into the sea. At 0·30a.m., the artillery fire ceased.

General Fernández had neither communication with headquarters nor a radio link with the unit commanders, having to send paper notes to them using messengers.

Batallón 2 and its reinforcements were ready to face the attack, with all their heavy weapons positioned facing the road to Central

Australia, being at the junction of this road, the road to Playa Girón and the entrance to Playa Larga, which was like a triangular-shaped roundabout. The forces received from Batallón 4 were stationed on the beach, to prevent any attempt by the enemy to approach from the sea, while those of Batallón 6 were placed between the road junction and the beach.

They waited until Castro's forces were very close to open fire, using all their weapons and halting the advance completely, killing around 15 men in the first clash. The troops of Columna José Martí soon reached the Escuela de Responsables de Milicias and the units started to fight together, but were impeded in their advance towards Playa Larga by heavy enemy fire.

Then four T-34s (one was left at Pálpite with the headquarters, to be used to communicate orders for the tanks) appeared, advancing to the road junction, followed by infantry, and the Brigade's M-41 had to retreat. The four tanks lost communication between themselves, and the infantry moved to the sides of the road, hiding in the vegetation and advancing very slowly. The commander of the tanks, Néstor López Cuba, was with the first tank and decided to try to enter the town, firing his gun against the enemy as he went and receiving heavy fire from all kind of weapons. His T-34 was immediately hit on a track by an anti-tank weapon and went off the road into a ditch. Despite being out of service, the tank kept using its machine gun, so Brigade infantry fired on it with a machine gun, using the tracers to let a man with a bazooka fire at the tank. However, the second T-34 then fired at and killed the man with the bazooka and wounded the commander of F Company of Batallón 2, Máximo Cruz.

López Cuba managed to abandon his tank after the gun was damaged and crept to the second tank under enemy fire, but then that tank started to receive heavy fire and he jumped out and went to the

Men of the Milicias moving Soviet-built BS-3 M1944 100mm howitzers into position.

Soviet-built M1937 (ML-20) 152mm guns used by Cuban forces to fire against the positions of the Brigade.

M1937 (ML-20) 152mm howitzers being towed close to Bahía de Cochinos.

M1937 (ML-20) 152mm howitzers used by the Milicias Nacionales Revolucionarias and Fuerzas Armadas Revolucionarias.

A truck moves close to Bahía de Cochinos area, armed with a Soviet-built DShK-M 12.7×108mm machine gun.

third tank. According to López Cuba, to avoid being destroyed, the second tank moved backwards and crashed into the third one. Some sources state that in fact they were hit by the M-41, which later fired upon the tank, destroying it.[49] López Cuba ordered his tank crew to move back too and then passed the second tank to their right, advancing and firing the main gun and machine guns until reaching the road junction. López Cuba tried to return to his damaged tank for the crew, but he was wounded and evacuated to Central Australia.

The second tank was destroyed by anti-tank weapons and only one crewmember survived.

The militia at one time sent an ambulance under a white flag to pick up the wounded, but tried to sneak two trucks loaded with militia in behind it. The tank destroyed all three vehicles with one round and its machine guns.

According to Grayston Lynch,[50] a second attack was made by T-34s and, in total, six were knocked out. Finally, at 3:00 a.m., the tank attacks ceased and a big infantry attack was launched, but was received by heavy fire from infantry, tanks and mortars.

At around 4:45 a.m., the M-41 was out of ammunition and pulled back, but the mortars and recoilless guns kept firing for the rest of the night, until, by 5:30 a.m., Castro's forces started to pull back. By early morning, it was clear that the forces of Brigade 2506 had been successful containing the attack. General Fernández was informed of the arrival at Pálpite of Battalions 123, 144 and 180 of the militia coming from La Habana, but he decided to retire the Escuela de Responsables de Milicias and Columna 1 to remain as a reserve and

recover from the battle. At dawn, 10 extra T-34 tanks arrived from Central Australia, followed later by some SUU-100 casemate tanks and IS-2M heavy tanks, which were all moved during the night to avoid being attacked by enemy aviation.

During the nigfht clash, Batallón 2 had lost 20 men and 50 wounded, but despite being triumphant, they were running out of ammunition and they knew that Castro's forces would shortly resume the attack. As

49 *The Bay of Pigs, Cuba 1961*, Alejandro de Quesada, Osprey Publishing, Oxford, 2009.

50 *Decision for Disaster, Betrayal at the Bay of Pigs*, Grayston Lynch, Brassey', Dulles, VA, 1998.

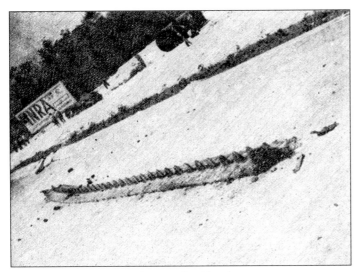

The tracks of the first T-34 destroyed at Playa Larga.

Troops of the Milicias and Fuerzas Armadas Revolucionarias. They are armed with the Czechoslovak Sa.25 sub-machine gun.

An M-43 120mm heavy mortar used by the Rebel Army and militia.

The militia sent an ambulance under a white flag to pick up wounded but tried to sneak two trucks loaded with militia troops behind it. An M-41 destroyed all three vehicles, the ambulance being hit by machine-gun fire.

Without supplies

Meanwhile, at Playa Girón, the ships had left and many of the supplies had not been landed, and Pérez San Román lost contact with the cargo ships, as the communication truck was lost with the *Río Escondido*. The impossibility of wrenching control of the skies from the Cubans made things worse, as they were strafed by FAR planes.

The ships left the area despite San Román ordering them not to do so, leaving the force without the help of the ships' 75mm recoilless guns and anti-aircraft machine guns. Despite the plan being to return that night to continue offloading supplies, the *Caribe* and *Atlántico* left the area and it wasn't possible to make contact again with the *Blagar*. According to Grayston Lynch:[51]

After dark of D-Day we continued south hoping to make some contact with the cargo ships but to no avail. Sometime during the night a message was received directing the *Barbara J.* to unload her ammunition and a 500-man pack into one of the LCUs for a run into the beach that night. It was felt that the *Blagar* should go because of the damage the *Barbara J.* had sustained; however, upon charting the course we found that due to the slow speed of the LCU, we could not arrive until after daylight of D plus 1. Headquarters was notified of this and we were told not to go. While the planning for the run into the beach was underway, some of the crew of the

it was not possible to be resupplied, Erneido Oliva took the decision to retreat to Playa Girón and join the forces of San Román. At 7:30 a.m., they boarded their trucks - including many they had captured at Playa Larga after occupying the town - tanks and other vehicles and headed to Playa Girón, abandoning Playa Larga. They took their wounded with them but released all their prisoners on departure. They destroyed the radio station and all the trucks they could not use.

51 Grayston Lynch survey. National Defense University, Taylor Papers, Box 12, Cuba, Paramilitary Study. Secret; Eyes Only.

M30 122mm howitzers being fired against positions of the Brigade.

Cuban soldiers performing training with an M53 anti-aircraft gun, baptized "Cuatro Bocas", against a B-26C of the Fuerza Aérea Revolucionaria.

Soldiers of the Fuerzas Armadas Revolucionarias firing against enemy forces using Vz-52 Czechoslovak rifles.

Men of the militia operating an M53 anti-aircraft gun, baptized "Cuatro Bocas", near Bay of Pigs.

Rio Escondido that we had rescued went into the engine room and stopped the engines. They said they would not go back into the beach area without jet air cover. They were subdued and the engines were started again. Some of the Cuban crew of the *Blagar* were in sympathy with them and there were some rumors of mutiny.

US Navy destroyers intercepted the *Atlántico* 110 nautical miles south of the beachhead and convinced her captain to return, but she could not arrive in the area again until 6.30 p.m. on D+1, 18 April. The *Caribe* was not overtaken by a destroyer until she was 218 miles south, and was not available to resupply the Brigade before the beachhead collapsed.[52]

During the second half of the 17th, the forces at Playa Girón saw no major actions, despite knowing the enemy was assembling at Covadonga and Yaguaramas. Batallion 111 of the Milicias drove the paratroopers from Jocuma to Canal de Muñoz. Battalion 111 did not keep up their advance, and preparations began to bomb the paratroopers with artillery and mortars. On the road from Yaguaramas, the two companies of Battalion 117 were reinforced by Battalion 113, but made no significant progress before nightfall.

San Román deployed part of his forces to blockade the road to Playa Larga and others on the road to Cienfuegos, while Batallón 1 was kept in their positions facing Covadonga and Yaguaramas.

The remains of a house completely destroyed at Playa Larga.

By nightfall, the 122mm artillery began firing against the forward troops of Batallón 1 who were near San Blas, and at 4:00 a.m. the artillery also opened fire against the forces at Playa Girón. Then an armoured column of troops - Batallón 111 of the Milicias from Covadonga - attacked the forces near San Blas, causing them to retreat, but Batallón 1 regrouped, together with a mortar unit, and waited for the chasing vehicles, opening fire against them once they

52 *The Bay of Pigs, Cuba 1961*, Alejandro de Quesada, Osprey Publishing, Oxford, 2009.

were in range and forcing them to retreat with many losses.

Almost at the same time, the troops of Batallón 1 near Horquitas contacted an enemy force they thought comprised four battalions and two armoured companies (in fact it was Batallón 117 of the Milicias, a Police battalion and some tanks), opening fire against the vanguard of the enemy column and forcing it to retreat. After that, they moved to a

position closer to San Blas, to be nearer the main forces of the Brigade and to sustain the expected attack on the 18th.

San Román spent the night waiting for the ships, with a group of men on the beach ready to receive the load, but no ships appeared. He tried to make contact with the ships and even sent a boat to the bay to try to establish radio contact, but without success.

CHAPTER 9
DEFENDING PLAYA GIRÓN

From Playa Larga to Girón

Around 9:00 a.m., the forces of Brigade 2506 were concentrated at Playa Girón, when Batallón 2 and its reinforcements arrived from Playa Larga. Erneido Oliva expected that supplies had been delivered at Playa Girón during the night, but this wasn't the case. His troops were tired after the night battle, they knew they were going to be attacked at Playa Larga during the day and that they didn't have enough ammunition to sustain a new assault. Once they arrived to Playa Girón, they were positioned defending the road from Playa Larga, while the main forces of San Román were facing San Blas. Only a small advanced force of Batallón 4 was kept on the road to Cienfuegos, with two of the M-41 tanks, as they did not detect any enemy in that direction, and Batallón 3 was sent to San Blas to operate under the command of the commander of Batallón 1.

On the morning of the 18 April, the troops of Batallón 1 were defending the roads to San Blas against units coming from Covadonga and Yaguaramas, keeping them at a distance mainly by employing their mortars, while also mounting a minor attack using tanks and infantry, until they ran out of ammunition and retreated to their positions at San Blas. During the day they positioned themselves at La Ceiba, close to San Blas. Around midday, the 122mm artillery under Commander Pedro Miret opened fire against their positions, making the situation very tough for them, and they were ordered to retreat to San Blas and join Batallón 3. Castro was preparing an attack against them, which would be made with 10 IS-2 tanks, five T-34s and five battalions, two of them acting as reserve.

San Román and Oliva met to organize their resistance, as it was clear that the enemy at Pálpite and Central Australia would advance, following the road from Playa Larga to Playa Girón. All their forces were low on ammunition and they needed supplies fast. Oliva suggested trying to move to the east in an attempt to break the enemy positions there and try to reach the Escambray mountains, but San Román was against the idea of abandoning a conventional fight for guerrilla warfare. He thought that, if they could receive supplies the following night, they could resist. San Román also explained to Oliva that he had faith that the United States government would not abandon them.[53] "My thought was that something went wrong and that the government machinery had locked," he explained, adding that at 10:30 a.m. they made contact with Grayston Lynch on the *Blagar*, and he was informed they would be supplied that night by LCUs and air drops. He was also told that if things went very badly, they would be evacuated by the ships.

Another reason for not going to the Escambray hills was that, as the road to Cienfuegos was empty of enemies, it smelled like a trap, as if Castro had decided to leave it empty to tempt them to escape along

A view from an FAL B-26 while attacking a troop column of the Ejército Rebelde and Milicias Revolucionarias that was moving from Playa Larga to Playa Girón on 18 April.

The Leyland buses, full of troops, were an easy target for the B-26s of the FAL. They were also attacked by mistake by the FAR. The number of casualties is still unknown.

53 *Respuesta. La verdad sobre Girón*, Comandante José Pérez San Román, Miami, Florida, 1979.

One of the Leyland buses destroyed on the road to Playa Girón on 18 April.

A soldier of the militia on the remains of the B-26B of Matías Farías at Playa Girón airfield.

Soldiers of Brigada 2506 with Johnson M1941 .30-06 rifles with telescopic sights.

it and then be ambushed and destroyed. After he was captured, San Román was told by Castro that this indeed was his plan, and he had deployed Batallón 326's 400 men to wait for the Brigade in that area.

As soon as dawn came, General José Ramón Fernández sent battalions 123 and 180 (under command of Lieutenant Jacinto Vázquez de la Garza) to resume the attack on Playa Larga, one of them approaching along the road to Pálpite and the other from the west, through the nearby town of Buenaventura, while Batallón 144 was finding its way from Soplillar to the coast, to attack Playa Larga from the east. Castro ordered the 10 T-34s that arrived in the night, the

two surviving tanks from the night battle and some SUU-100s to go to Soplillar and then to the coast to attack Playa Larga from the east with Batallón 144, but he was informed that the commander of the SUU-100s needed about two hours to make them ready for battle, as some needed repairs.

When the troops were approaching Playa Larga at 8:00 a.m, a group of civilians with white flags approached and informed them that the enemy had left. When Castro was informed about this, around 11:45 a.m., he went into a rage, furious that the enemy had escaped. He ordered Fernández to keep advancing towards Playa Girón and to chase the retreating enemy, while the FAR was also to attack them.

At 12:00 p.m., Fernández prepared Batallón 123 and ordered them to go to Playa Girón, with six SUU-100 tanks in the lead and the troops walking behind in combat formation. Part of a company would be on the tanks and they would be protected by two batteries of Cuatro Bocas AAA. But before the troops left, he received an urgent order from Castro, informing him that the enemy had been defeated and was on the run, and he was to chase them as fast as he could. At 12:15 p.m., he received orders from headquarters saying: "We have to take Playa Girón before 6:00 p.m." An officer leading a forward patrol then returned, informing him there was no trace of any enemy on the first 14-16km of the road.

Accordingly, General Fernández changed his orders and decided to send the troops on board the Leyland buses they used to arrive at Pálpite, forming a column with the tanks in front and the Cuatro

An M1939 61-K automatic 37mm anti-aircraft gun being towed close to Bahía de Cochinos during the action.

Men of Brigade 2506 during training, using a recoilless gun. They were very effective against Castro's tanks and other vehicles.

Militia firing over the roofs of houses. One is already armed with a Kalashnikov AK-47 rifle.

A concentration of troops of Batallón 123 at Playa Larga, with SUU-100 self-propelled guns. They were sent to Playa Girón to try to defeat the enemy before nightfall. The troops went on board the Leyland buses they used to arrive at Pálpite, forming a column with the tanks in front and the Cuatro Bocas guns being towed at the rear. Before reaching Playa Girón, they were bombed by the planes of both sides and the battalion was almost completely annihilated.

Air operations

Early in the morning, at 5:00 a.m., the FAR pilots were called by their commander, Raúl Curbelo (then Communications Minister, sent by Castro to take control of the FAR in place of Commander Guerra Bermejo, and nicknamed "Maro", as he had no knowledge of how to command the aviation), to organize the day's missions. He explained that they would have to provide support to the ground forces and prevent any attempt by the Brigade's ships to deliver more supplies. The first action would be to bomb Playa Larga in the morning with two planes, with Alberto Fernández and Ernesto Guerrero (a Nicaraguan pilot, on his first combat mission) in T-33s, while a Sea Fury with Enrique Carreras bombed the *Houston* again, as people were spotted on board. The planes were to depart at 6:15 a.m.

Fernández and Guerrero each dropped their two 250kg bombs over the town of Playa Larga, but without causing casualties to Brigade forces. According to Carreras Rolas,[55] Álvaro Galo also took part in the mission with a B-26, with Juan Suárez Plaza as navigator, Adriano Sánchez as flight mechanic and Pedro Delgado Lugo as tail gunner. Rolas said that Galo bombed the airfield at Playa Girón, but his bombs did not hit the runway, then he strafed a truck and an AAA position

Bocas guns being towed in the rear.

In the meantime, at 12:15 p.m., Castro asked the airfield at Baracoa how many helicopters they had operational there, with the idea of sending a company of Batallón 122 from Yaguaramas, specially equipped with rocket launchers, to a place on the road between San Blas and Playa Girón. According to Castro,[54] they had three transport helicopters (S-55s or Whirlwinds) operational.

54 *La Batalla de Girón*, Fidel Castro Ruz, La Habana, 2011.

55 *Por el dominio del aire*, Enrique Carreras Rolas, Editora Política, La Habana 2008.

Two SUU-100 self-propelled guns and a T-34 tank close to Playa Larga.

Militia and Army soldiers marching, armed with Super-Bazooka M20 rocket launchers.

Fidel Castro inspecting a Cuatro Bocas anti-aircraft gun during the fighting.

before returning to San Antonio de los Baños. In his book, Jacques Lagas says that he was the pilot of that plane and that it was the FAR serialled 915.[56] Lagas also states that, by then, the B-26s with serials 909, 915 and 917 had received bombings sights, which they did not previously have, and that the 937 was also in service. Carreras then attacked the *Houston* with bombs, rockets and his guns, after which he heard Guerrero saying he was hit and there was smoke in his cockpit. Carreras escorted him back to base, as he was losing hydraulic pressure and had to lower the landing gear manually. The T-33, serialled 703, remained out of service, leaving only the 709 and 711 operational.

Lagas states that he attacked enemy machine gun positions at the junction of the road from San Blas to Girón and that which goes to Cayo Ramona. He dropped four bombs on enemy positions, while the rear gunner strafed them, despite receiving anti-aircraft fire from both the enemy and their own troops.

As soon as Fernández and Guerrero returned, Prendes and Del Pino received their mission to attack the runway at Playa Girón again, the first flying the 709 and the latter the 711. When they were approaching the area, Prendes spotted a B-26 and went to attack it, but he then saw the transparent nose, realizing it was Galo's plane, and aborted the interception. Both T-33s then dropped the bombs over the airfield, but without causing much damage to the runway. Prendes dropped one bomb on each dive and made a strafing pass after that, being hit and returning to base with low hydraulic pressure, making an emergency landing.

At almost the same time, and unnoticed by the FAR crews, two US Navy A-4Bs made a flight over the area. The *Blagar* informed the pair not to fire on them; they believed they were going to attack FAR planes or Cuban ground troops, raising hopes that the US government had finally decided to intervene and save the invasion. However, Grayston Lynch was informed by the USS *Essex* that the planes were only to perform a reconnaissance mission.

In the meantime, at Puerto Cabezas, a strike mission to support the ground troops was organized with six planes, but as the Cuban crews were extremely tired and with morale very low after so many losses during the previous days, the US government authorized that US pilots could fly two of the planes. The B-26s would use the callsigns Chico (serials 965 with René García and Luis Ardois and 950 with Mario Zuñiga and Manuel Villafaña), Tigre (955 with Antonio Soto and Benito González and 960 with Gustavo Ponzoa and Rafael García Pujol) and Lobo (945 with Connie Seigrist - under the code name Simpson - with Gustavo Villoldo and 927 with Doug Price - another CIA pilot, with the code name Peters - and Alberto Pérez Sordo).

They took off at 2:00 p.m. and headed to Bay of Pigs, having been informed of the advance of Batallón 123 of the Milicias towards Playa Girón. The six bombers found the column on its way from Playa Larga, at Punta Perdiz. The ground troops cheered them, thinking they were FAR planes, but the B-26s launched their air strike, bombing and strafing the buses and tanks, using napalm for the first time in the operation.

Connie Seigrist recalls the mission as follows:[57]

I informed my Agency boss (Gar Thorsrud) that I would like to take a flight to give aerial support for our now stranded ground troops. He granted permission provided there be at least one Cuban flown B-26 with each American flown B-26. Capt. Price decided to fly. We accounted for the first two American flown B-26s in the invasion. Four Cuban B-26 crews immediately volunteered to go with us as they also felt the ground troops should not be left to forage for themselves. […] A blue stripe on ground equipment, aircraft, or laid on the ground during the invasion was our identification. Anything in Cuba not showing a blue stripe or panel was fair game. We six aircraft departed Puerto Cabezas and arrived over Bay of Pigs about an hour before dark. We spread, armed our switches, and test fired our guns when the coast was coming in sight. My aircraft carried eight 225lb fragmentation bombs, eight fragmentation

56 *Memorias de un capitán rebelde*, Jacques Lagas, Editorial Del Pacífico, Santiago de Chile, 1964.

57 *Memoirs*, Connie Seigrist, University of Texas Dallas, William M. Leary Papers, Box 11 Folder 9.

Men of the militia and the Army at Playa Larga, ready to march to Playa Girón.

A photographer stands beside one of the Leyland buses bombed between Playa Larga and Playa Girón.

rockets, and fully armed fourteen forward firing .50 cal guns.[58] Some others carried napalm. As we were coming over the coast I could see a convoy of vehicles coming from inland down the only road toward the beach. I knew our invading troops did not have enough ground equipment to form a convoy plus no blue stripes were visible. I decided to go straight in opening my bomb-bay doors while lining up for my dive. I set the intervalometer to release all bombs equally spaced within four seconds. When lined up on the lead tank I started my dive. When in range I released the bombs and simultaneously held down on my firing trigger while flying down the entire convoy. I turned out immediately making a 270 degree turn to come back in crosswise of the convoy to fire my rockets. I released two rockets at the tanks and watched as they ricochet [sic] of[f] the tanks exploding into the air. I then joined pattern behind my flight. I then came around again in turn this time to fire my remaining rockets into the last three trucks in line that were towing field artillery pieces. My stores were now expended except for a few rounds of .50s for emergency and I pulled out to fly watch while the other B-26s completed their runs. We left the area as the last aircraft pulled up. The convoy looked awfully messed up as we departed, but I had my doubts that we caused much damage to the tanks. Doug's trim system had been shot and he was having some control difficulties. I encouraged him to drop his tanks. He tried but they kept hanging on. He finally managed to get his aircraft under control. All of us took a few rounds, but no real damage and no one was injured. Later we were informed two Castro T-33s arrived over the area in less than a minute after we departed from our strike. We arrived back over Puerto Cabezas after dark. A couple of Cuban B-26s were very low on fuel. A flight of replacement B-26s from Field Three had arrived shortly before us. While landing they had run into some grazing ponies that had gotten on to the runway and the runway was closed until the ground crews could remove the bodies. It was a touch and go situation. Luckily the ponies were removed in a short time and the aircraft without much fuel remaining made it for landing just as the crew were positioning to bail out.

This was the only truly successful attack performed by the Fuerza Aérea de Liberación, as they destroyed the ground target without suffering losses.

Almost at the same time as this attack, the FAR received orders from Castro to attack the retreating Batallón 2 on its way to Playa Girón, and many sorties were flown with the T-33 serialled 711, two

Sea Furies and the FAR B-26 serialled 909 (according to Carreras, a total of 20 sorties were flown in the day, while Del Pino states there were more than 25). The planes were ordered to attack any troop concentration from Soplillar to Playa Girón. According to Del Pino,[59] they also attacked by mistake the troops of Batallón 123, as they were the only troops on that road, with Prendes saying he made two strike missions, on one of them destroying a truck. Bourzac also said he made a strike mission, but was hit before reaching the target and, due to electrical failures caused by the impact, h had to drop the bombs in salvo and return to base with the eight rockets still hanging from their pylons, with the risk of being fired at any moment. Lagas said that at 4:10 p.m., he took off with the FAR B-26 serialled 917, but smoke in the cockpit forced him to return and make an emergency landing.[60]

A huge amount of casualties resulted from the attack on the Brigade by the FAR planes, but the final number varies according to the source, from about 100 to more than 1,000 (this last number is exaggerated, as the column only had around 900 men).

Attack delayed

The almost complete destruction of Batallón 123 led to the decision to postpone the attack on Playa Girón until the next morning. Around sunset, Castro again arrived at the area of operations, this time at Covadonga, to direct the attack personally, as he believed General Fernández was not progressing as fast as he could.

During the afternoon, an exploration force from Playa Larga commanded by Orlando Pupo Peña reached the advanced positions of Batallón 2 to the north of Playa Girón, coming under fire and suffering three men killed. Shortly after their arrival, a Whirlwind helicopter arrived with three men with rocket launchers; as it wasn't possible to get more helicopters, the small force could not be deployed between San Blas and Playa Girón as planned.

At 6:00 p.m., the artillery, particularly the 122mm guns, opened fire against the positions at San Blas, but later started to shell the entire area that Brigade 2506 was still holding. They kept shelling them for the whole night, preparing the field for an assault on the morning of 19 April.

After sunset, a battalion of the Policía Nacional Revolucionaria approached Playa Girón along the road from Playa Larga, under the command of Efigenio Ameijeiras, to take the place of the destroyed Batallón 123.

San Román expected an attack from the road to Playa Larga

58 As Seigrist stated, the planes received during the invasion also had four extra machine guns on the wings, but this made a total of 12, not 14 as he states in his book. This plane was probably one of those received during the 17th.

59 *9050 Horas*, Rafael del Pino, Miami, 2012.

60 *Memorias de un capitán rebelde*, Jacques Lagas, Editorial Del Pacífico, Santiago de Chile, 1964.

at nightfall and prepared Batallón 2 there, but the attack never materialized and only a few skirmishes occurred during the night on this front and around San Blas.

The main problem for the Brigade was that they were running out of ammunitions and food, and they expected a big attack from all directions during the night or on the 19th.

Sending supplies

Brigade 2506 needed supplies desperately and, due to the distance the ships were from the coast at that time, the only way to do it was by air. The ships would have to arrive at the beach shortly before sunrise and perform part of the landing in daylight, under the threat of FAR planes. The *Atlántico* had transferred part of its cargo to the *Barbara J.*, the *Blagar* and the LCUs, but they would not arrive until sunrise, as they were so far from the beach. The only way to resupply faster was by plane, and Eduardo Ferrer said that in the afternoon three C-54s were to be sent to airdrop supplies over the beach, with the callsign Halcón. He would be the leader (on the plane serialled 7107), with Mario Tellechea in Halcón 2 (7711) and Castor Cereceda in Halcón 3 (7710). They took off at 3:30 p.m., and shortly before 7:00 p.m. were approaching Playa Girón.

They flew at 400ft to avoid being detected by the enemy until over the target, and then they climbed to 800ft to make the drop. Once they passed over the town they were fired on by AAA from Castro's forces. According to Grayston Lynch:[61]

> We were told that several air drops were to be made on the night of D plus 1 on the air field and the brigade was notified and marked the strip. The first air drop on the field was made but most of the chutes drifted off the strip into the woods. (These were recovered the next morning.) The brigade then requested that the drops be made on the town itself and the two later drops that night went there; one of them was right on target and the supplies landed in the streets and were quickly recovered[,] but the last one was too close to the water and most of the chutes drifted into the sea. Some of these were recovered by small boats later on.

61 Grayston Lynch survey. National Defense University, Taylor Papers, Box 12, Cuba, Paramilitary Study. Secret; Eyes Only.

A bar completely destroyed at Playa Larga. The fight for the town between 17-and 18 April was the fiercest of the whole battle.

As the situation of the Brigade became critical, the Nicaraguan government decided to offer six P-51D Mustangs to provide air cover for the planes. The first idea was to send them to protect two C-46s that would land at Playa Girón airfield with supplies, but this mission was cancelled. Later, it was decided to protect a flight of B-26s over the beach on 19 April, when the plan was to launch an air strike to try to destroy as many enemy troops as possible to stop the attack on the Brigade and win some time until the forces on the beach could be resupplied. The problem was that there were no Cubans trained on the model and no Nicaraguan pilots were allowed to fly them.

During the night, a meeting took place at the White House in Washington DC to decide the actions that must be taken to save the invasion. Admiral Arleigh Burke, Chief of Naval Operations of the US Navy, tried to convince President Kennedy to take action and destroy Castro's forces using US military power. Kennedy still tried to maintain the facade of not being involved, and only authorized air cover by two Douglas A-4B Skyhawks for one hour during the morning, with the intention of being over the area at the same time as the planned B-26 attacks. But again, the Skyhawks were not authorized to fire unless they were fired upon.

CHAPTER 10

DEFEAT

Air strikes in the morning

The success of the air strikes on 18 April and the need to give urgent support to the troops on the beach led to the planning of a new series of sorties for the early morning of the 19th by the Fuerza Aérea de Liberación. Most of the Cuban pilots were exhausted from the missions they had flown, which were very long, and others were scared of the presence of fighters, so spirits for the new missions were very low. To add to the Cuban flyers, US pilots were asked if they wanted to volunteer. Hal McGee, Riley Shamburger, Thomas (Pete) Ray, Dalton Livingston, Billy Goodwin and Connie Seigrist offered to go, along with Cuban pilots Gonzalo Herrera and Mario Zuñiga. US pilots Leo Baker, Wade Gray, Joe Shannon, Nick Sudano and James Vaughn also later volunteered, and crews were assembled with two US pilots on each B-26, while one of the US pilots flew with Mario Zuñiga as navigator. Gray would fly with Shamburger, and Baker with Ray,

while Shannon and Sudano would fly together and Seigrist with Doug Price. Zuñiga and Vaughn flew as navigators for Goodwin, Livingston or Mc Gee, but it wasn't determined who was flying with whom.

All eight available B-26s would be used on this mission.

Gonzalo Herrera and Goodwin were the first to take off, the former with an unknown navigator who fled from the plane before take-off. They took off at 1:00 a.m. to attack the road from Girón to Cienfuegos, while they would also protect a C-46, commanded by Captain Manuel Navarro and José Pellón, that would try to land at Girón airfield to leave a load of ammunition. They arrived to Girón at dawn and the C-46 managed to land, leaving its four tons of cargo; they were told by the Brigade's doctor, Dr Juan Sordo, that he had many wounded men to be evacuated, but to move them to the plane would take up to two hours. This would be enough time for the FAR fighters to destroy the C-46 on the ground or when leaving, so Navarro decided to take

A T-34 tank advancing near the beaches at Girón.

The remains of Shamburguer's B-26 near Central Australia.

A T-34 near Playa Larga, from where Cuban forces advanced towards Girón.

only pilot Matías Farias, who was shot down on the 17th and seriously wounded, as he was already on the airfield, and took off.

Both B-26s bombed a convoy of tanks and trucks approaching Girón in the area of San Blas, destroying some of them with napalm and rockets, but Goodwin was unable to fire his machine guns and returned with a rocket hanging from the wing pylon nose-down. After many unsuccessful attempts to dislodge the rocket, he had to land with it; fortunately it did not explode.

After the B-26 of Herrera took off from Puerto Cabezas, the planes of Shamburger and Ray followed at 2:45 a.m., heading for Girón. It was believed that between 6:30-7:30 a.m. there would be four A-4B Skyhawks, commanded by Mike Griffin, providing air cover for the B-26s, but when the bombers arrived they saw none of them.

The C-54 with serial 7711, with a US crew, was also sent to make an airdrop of supplies over the beach at dawn, but they returned before reaching the target.

Fifteen minutes after Shamburger and Ray, Shannon and McGee took off, and the four planes approached Girón together. They were followed by Livingston and Seigrist, who took off at 4:30 a.m.[62]

In the meantime, at San Antonio de los Baños, the first missions of the day were being prepared, with Álvaro Prendes to fly the T-33 serialled 709 and Enrique Carreras Rolas on the 711, with callsigns Granma and Frank respectively, to patrol the skies to the south of Girón in search of enemy bombers and any ships approaching the

area. Flying at 10,000ft, they saw two US destroyers approaching Bay of Pigs and continued flying, looking for the landing craft and transports, until Carreras saw the four B-26s approaching Girón at less than 3,000ft. Ray then said over the radio "Going in", indicating they were to begin their attack. Carreras turned towards the four planes and saw the two that were to the left breaking formation and turning fast, while the pair to the right continued flying ahead. Prendes ordered Carreras to go for the one to the left of that pair and he went for the other; apparently they were the planes of Shamburger and Ray. Carreras fired at his B-26 when he was very close, hitting the fuselage and the left wing and engine. According to some accounts, the pilot - identified by some of the other pilots of the mission as Shamburger - managed to shout over the radio "Hit, hit!", but that was the last that was heard from him. Prendes says he did the same with the other plane, approaching slowly and opening fire once he was very close, damaging the fuselage and the left wing and engine. The plane exploded and fell into the sea. The FAR pilots claimed to have shot down both B-26s, one being that of Shamburger and the other being Ray's, and both Cubans described their "kill" falling into the sea.

Some Cuban sources indicate that Shamburger's plane was in fact shot down by AAA near Central Australia after the B-26 made several attacks on the troops there, including three strafing passes. Troops on

62 According to Albert Persons, McGee was flying with Shamburger and Shannon with Ray, but the two Cuban pilots that intercepted them said the planes of Shamburger and Ray were flying in formation to the right and the other two were to the left, and turned as soon as they saw the T-33s approaching. See *Bay of Pigs, a first hand account of the mission by a U.S. pilot in support of the Cuban Invasion Force of 1961*, Albert C. Persons, McFarland & Company, North Carolina, 1990. The CIA report *Official history of the Bay of Pigs Operation*, Jack Pfeiffer, Central Intelligence Agency, 1979, states that Shamburger and Shannon were on the same escadrille, together with Ray, and doesn't include McGee as flying that day.

An M1939 61-K 37mm automatic anti-aircraft gun with men of the Milicias in the area of combat, most probably near Central Australia, where most of the anti-aircraft guns were placed to protect the command post and where Shamburguer's plane was shot down.

Two of the 10 IS-2 heavy tanks deployed to Playa Larga together with five T-34s. The M-41 was an easy target for them, but when they arrived at the town the Brigade had already retreated to Girón and they were not used in combat.

Men of the Milicias and the Army deploying to Girón. The truck is armed with an M53 anti-aircraft gun

Troops of the Milicias advancing beside a T-34 tank towards Girón.

the ground saw the plane being hit in the fuselage and right engine before falling. Leo Baker survived the crash, which occurred close to Central Australia, and left the plane with his gun, only to be killed shortly after by the militia.

Carreras and Prendes possibly both fired on Ray's plane, as the description of how his plane fell is very similar in both cases; especially interesting is that both describe the plane they shot down as falling into the sea, while Shamburger's plane crashed into the ground.

While this action was happening, the planes of Shannon and McGee were very close to those of Shamburger and Ray, but they continued with their mission. While they were pressing their attacks

against ground targets to the east of Girón, both pilots saw the T-33s and fled. When they were leaving the area, they saw two A-4Bs from the USS *Essex* heading north; there was a misunderstanding of the time they were to provide air cover, and they were just arriving in the area of operations. After hearing of the loss of the two B-26s, Seigrist and Livingston decided to return to base before reaching Girón.

At the same time that the attack of the B-26s was taking place, an unknown C-46, piloted by Captain Gómez, flew to Girón, but was recalled due to the presence of enemy fighters. The C-46 serialled 864, piloted by Captain Luaices, also flew to Girón airfield, but the landing was aborted.

With the intention of trying to recover the downed crews, the Brigade PBY Catalina was used as radio relay and SAR aircraft approached the Bay of Pigs and conducted a search, despite their orders to stay outside the 12-mile limit of Cuban waters. They get as close as a mile from the shore, at 200ft, but found nothing.

While this was happening, six North American P-51D Mustangs were made available by the Fuerza Aérea de Nicaragua to provide fighter escort for the B-26s. Albert Persons, who had experience on the model, had been asked to select five Cuban pilots and train them on the model, to fly on 19 April to Girón, the planes armed with rockets and machine guns and equipped with extra fuel tanks. They would have to land on the airfield and start close air support operations from there, with supplies for them being delivered by plane or landing craft. Persons realized the Cuban pilots had very little experience of flying a single-engined fighter, the Sea Fury, but one of them had none. When they were ready to take off for Cuba after lunch, they were told to cancel the operation.

Another idea was to drop fuel tanks loaded with napalm from a C-54, but this idea was also cancelled after some drums were loaded

Trucks progressing to Girón carrying troops.

M53 anti-aircraft guns in position on a road to protect the vehicles against the air strikes.

on the plane.

Attack sorties by the FAR

According to Lagas, he performed an attack sortie with the FAR B-26 serialled 915 after the plane was repaired from hits received on the previous day's mission. He approached Playa Girón and was met by a large amount of AAA, but managed to drop his bombs and return safely.[63]

The next sortie to be flown by the FAR was planned with the two serviceable T-33s (serials 709 and 711), flown by Alberto Fernandez and Rafael del Pino, and two Sea Furies with Douglas Rudd and Gustavo Bourzac. Their mission was to attack the ground troops at Girón and its surroundings. Arriving in the area, they noted a lot of AAA from their own forces, but firing against any plane. They dropped their ordnance over the enemy troops and returned to base. After this mission, Del Pino flew again with Álvaro Prendes, in the two T-33s, the former in the 711 and the latter the 709. According to Prendes, they had expended all the rockets for the planes, so they were only armed with machine guns. He also stated that there were just a few 250lb bombs remaining in their stocks.[64] They noticed a lot of troops on the beach, with boats going from there to a US destroyer that was close to the coast, and they went to attack the boats, fearing the destroyer would open fire upon them, although they saw no tracers coming from the ship. Prendes attacked first, followed by Del Pino,

and they immediately went for another pass. After that, both pilots attacked the beach and were joined by a pair of Sea Furies, flown by Rudd and Bourzac, who were flying their second mission of the day. After expending all their ammunition, the four planes returned to San Antonio de los Baños. Lagas declared that he performed his second mission of the day on the FAR B-26 serialled 909, departing at 1:00 p.m. and bombing a mortar position between the airfield and Playa Girón.[65]

When they landed and informed their commander, Curbelo, what they had seen, they realized that the Brigade was evacuating the beach, so the order was given to organize a major attack on them with all available planes. Two Sea Furies, the pair of T-33s and two B-26s were prepared (Carreras said that they were the 909 and 917, and that the 915 was also in flying condition but that only two flew,[66] while Prendes in his book stated that there were three B-26s on this mission). Carreras flew in a B-26 with Sergeant Domingo Martínez González as mechanic, Cadet Víctor Hernández Sanchez as navigator and Raúl Calzado Ramos as gunner. He said that in the other plane was Lagas with Eloy Vera Vento as mechanic, Pedro Delgado Lugo as gunner and Cadet Juan Suárez Plaza as navigator. Bourzac and Rudd were in the Sea Furies, with Fernández and Prendes in the T-33s.

They took off at 3:45 p.m. and headed for Playa Girón, but Carreras' B-26 had smoke in the cabin caused by a fire somewhere on the plane,

63 *Memorias de un capitán rebelde*, Jacques Lagas, Editorial Del Pacífico, Santiago de Chile, 1964.

64 *En el punto rojo de mi kolimador. Crónicas de un aviador*, Álvaro Prendes, Editorial Letras Cubanas, La Habana, 1982.

65 *Memorias de un capitán rebelde*, Jacques Lagas, Editorial Del Pacífico, Santiago de Chile, 1964.

66 *Por el dominio del aire*, Enrique Carreras Rolas, Editora Política, La Habana 2008.

Trucks carrying M53 anti-aircraft guns moving to the area around Girón.

A truck full of Milicia soldiers during the fighting.

forcing them to return to base and make an emergency landing, while the other planes continued to their target. The other B-26 dropped its bombs on a levelled flight over the target, while the Sea Furies dived and fired rockets, dropped bombs and strafed the beach. After their attack, the two T-33s went in at very low level over the road to Playa Larga.

As soon as the planes returned, Carreras took off alone in one of the Sea Furies, which was armed with the bombs removed from his B-26 plus eight rockets. He bombed the runway of the airfield at Girón and then flew over two US destroyers that were close to the coast, while he saw what he describes as the USS *San Marcos* anchored near Cayo Guano, a small island about 45km to the south of Girón, then returned to base.

After Carreras landed, Fidel Castro ordered all air action to stop, as their troops were entering Playa Girón and the surrender was imminent.

Last ground battle

At sunrise, the forces at Covadonga - three battalions and an artillery group under the command of Commander Félix Duque - started their march to San Blas, but were stopped near Jocuma by fire from Battalions 1 and 3 and two of the M-41s. The attack was repelled and the Milicias retreated, but immediately after, the 122mm guns opened fire, forcing the disorganized retreat of Batallón 3, leading to the commander of Batallón 1, Alejandro del Valle, removing the commander of the other unit, Noelio Montero, replacing him with

Roberto San Román, brother of José San Román and commander of Batallón 4's heavy weapons.

Meanwhile, another force prepared its advance from Yaguaramas, to start at 9:00 a.m., with three battalions, eight T-34 tanks and a light company on board trucks, commanded by Captain Emilio Aragonés.

Along the road to Playa Larga also began the advance of Batallón 116 of the Milicias (led by Samuel Rodiles Planas) and the Batallón de la Policía Nacional Revolucionaria (under the command of Efigenio Ameijeiras), to which a company equipped with bazookas was added, after spending the night at Punta Perdices. Before their approach, around 9:00 a.m., four batteries of 122mm howitzers, one incomplete battery of 120mm mortars and two of 85mm guns shelled the positions of Batallón 6, which was defending the road, supported by Batallón 2 and one M-41. Initially, the 120mm mortars opened fire from a distance of 4.2km, followed by the howitzers, shelling the area from a distance of 3.8-4.8km.

Close to Girón, the vanguard of the advancing troops divided into two columns, one to the left of the road and the other between the beach and the road. As they approached the entrance to Girón, they were ambushed by Batallón 6 on a curve of the road, where the road from Playa Larga reaches Girón and another one forks at that point and circle the town. A major fire fight took place, with the Milicias and Police being catch in the open with no cover, suffering many casualties. They were also being fired on by the M-41 and two of the REO M-35 trucks with machine guns. The combat lasted the whole morning, with Castro's battalions progressing slowly towards Girón. The troops of the Brigade were well dug-in, waiting until their enemy was close to them to open fire, causing many casualties. After the battle began, San Román sent the M-41 that was defending the road to Cienfuegos to support them.

Five T-34s then appeared, and the Milicias and Police forces placed themselves behind them to cover their advance, but the Brigade troops still managed to hit many of the soldiers behind the tanks.

Two M-43 120mm heavy mortars used by Castro forces at Girón.

Ships of Task Force Alpha. They were sent to protect the Cuban exile force, but in the end were ordered to not take part in any action.

While progressing to the town, Captain Luis Carbó, in charge of the vanguard, was wounded in his left shoulder but kept fighting until he was hit in his face and killed.

According to Efigenio Ameijeiras, one of the T-34s was destroyed by a gun as soon as it turned the curve in the road, killing its crew and some of the infantry behind it. Immediately after, the second T-34 appeared and was also destroyed. Then, one of the five SUU-100 self-propelled guns fired and hit the M-41 commanded by Alemán, the second-in-command of the Tank Company of the Brigade, killing the entire crew. In this action at the curve, the crews of the machine guns mounted on the three M35A2 trucks were also killed, together with six men with rocket launchers. Erneido Oliva, in charge of Batallón 2, ordered the mortars to concentrate their fire on the area between the road and the sea to stop their advance, and then, at around 2:00 p.m., ordered a counter-attack by G Company of Batallón 2 with his remaining M-41, to recover the frontline, which had started to be broken by the enemy.

Shortly after, Ameijeiras received the order to retreat as the FAR was to make their air strike with the B-26s, Sea Furies and T-33s. Castro's forces in this area suffered a total of 38 men killed and more than 100 wounded.

At San Blas, the forces from Covadonga and Yaguaramas converged and applied more pressure on Batallóns 1 and 3. These troops received the air strike launched in the morning by the first planes of the Fuerza Aérea de Liberación, but according to the ground forces, they caused little damage. After reaching San Blas, the mortar fire against the battalions of the Milicias halted them until 10:00 a.m., when they resumed their attack with the support of the tanks, but the first T-34 to appear was destroyed by a gun, followed by a SUU-100 hit by a mortar which caused the extra fuel tanks to catch fire. Another tank was destroyed shortly after, but the forces of the Brigade also lost one of the M35A2 trucks armed with a 12.7mm machine gun and had to start retreating due to the superiority in numbers of their enemy. At 11:00 a.m. they had to abandon San Blas and took up defensive positions at El Helechal, a small town 6km from Playa Girón, but they were soon under fire from artillery and tanks, and at 2:00 p.m. they retreated to Playa Girón after resisting for more than two days in their positions.

The situation at Playa Girón was desperate, as the forces of Brigade 2506 were running out of ammunition and were told they would not receive any more until that night. At 3:00 p.m., San Román gathered the commanders of his battalions and ordered them to disengage and escape into the swamps organized in companies, avoiding contact

with the enemy, until "Uncle Sam arrives". After that, he made contact with Grayston Lynch, asking for support. Lynch replied that they could evacuate them with the LCUs and two LCIs, but San Román vowed to fight there until the end. Lynch said they were on their way, but still some hours away, and San Román replied that he had nothing to fight with; he was running out of ammunition, with enemy tanks in sight. Then he said he would destroy his communication equipment and left for the swamps with the intention of reaching the Escambray mountains.

Immediately after arrival, the troops that were fighting on the road to Playa Larga retreated after the air strikes by the FAR. They found tanks and many weapons abandoned and troops completely exhausted, some of them trying to reach the sea in small boats towards the destroyer the USS Eaton, which entered the bay to evaluate the situation on the beach

When Castro's forces approaching from Playa Larga saw the destroyers (the USS Murray had joined the Eaton) and the boats going to and from them, their commander, General José Ramón Fernandez, gathered his three T-34s, five SUU-100s, twelve 85mm guns and three Soviet-built half-track vehicles with recoilless guns and opened fire against the boats, with orders not to fire on the destroyers. Later, another twenty 85mm guns arrived and they opened fire too against the boats. Shortly after, the two destroyers moved out to sea, while their commanders deliberated if they should fire back or not.

At Playa Girón, Oliva organized a small force, including a single M-41, and took the road to Cienfuegos, but they were attacked by planes (they said there were two Sea Furies and one T-33, but there is no account of this attack on the Cuban side). At the same time, they were fired on by ground troops of Batallón 326, which damaged the track of the tank with a bazooka, leaving it unserviceable, and the troops disbanded and escaped to the swamps, being the last force of the Brigade to fight.

At 5:00 p.m., Fidel Castro arrived at El Helechal and ordered his troops to advance towards Playa Girón. At around 7:00 p.m., these troops and those coming from Playa Larga entered the town.

The efforts to carry supplies from the ships to the ground troops on the beach had continued on the night of 18 April. According to Grayston Lynch:

At about noon on D plus 2 the Blagar, the Barbara J. and the three LCUs loaded with supplies started for the beach. Our ETA

It's all over. Troops of Brigada 2506 surrender to Castro forces on 19 April.

The survivors of the Brigade were persecuted by the few helicopters of the FAR, including the few flyable Bell 47s.

After the actions, Fidel Castro went to Girón and a photo production was made of him simulating being in the front of battle, boarding and descending from tanks and other vehicles. Here, he is descending from a T-34 tank.

[Estimated Time of Arrival] was about 18:00 hours. At 13:00 I was told by the Navy and relayed to the brigade that close jet air support was coming. It never appeared. At 14:30 the brigade commander told me that he was out of contact with all units, out of ammunition, fighting in the water and under direct fire from tanks 500 yards away. He said he was destroying his equipment and heading for the woods. He then went off the air. At this time Headquarters was notified and the convoy reversed course as there was no need now for going in. One hour later a friendly PBY [Catalina] came from the direction of Blue Beach and passed us going Southwest.[67]

When Castro's troops reached the coast from the direction of El Helechal, they saw the two US destroyers recovering some troops of the Brigade that managed to escape on boats. Some of the troops wanted to fire against the destroyers, which would have given the US government an excuse to attack Cuba openly. The destroyers were aiming with their artillery at the coast and the Cubans first thought they were supporting a new landing, but they finally decided to hold their fire.

The Cubans had finally occupied Girón and the battle was won. Meanwhile, the Brigade's forces were trying to escape in the swamps, but none of them managed to reach the Escambray hills.

Evacuation and surrender

During the night of 19 April, the USS *Conway* approached the beach and recovered between 20 and 30 men of the Brigade who swam out, sending a boat to recover them.

67 Grayston Lynch survey. National Defense University, Taylor Papers, Box 12, Cuba, Paramilitary Study. Secret; Eyes Only.

The remains of the Brigade, after escaping to the swamps, were captured in the following days by Castro's troops, who raked the area to search for them with the support of helicopters. Some sources indicate they used Mi-1, Mi-2 and Mi-4 helicopters, but by that time the FAR only had a few Bell 47s and Whirlwinds operational. Some of the survivors of the Brigade managed to stay hidden for up to 11 days, but they had no food and were extremely exhausted after the actions, all being captured in the end.

Grayston Lynch states that:

On D plus 3 we received an order to take the UDT personnel left aboard the LCIs [three on *Blagar* and three on *Barbara J.*] and transfer them to the destroyer *Eaton* which was escorting us. This transfer was made using rubber UDT boats in very rough seas. Mr. Lynch and Mr. Robertson also transferred with the teams to lead them on the operation. The information we had indicated that the survivors of the *Houston* were on the west side of the Bay of Cochinos and were still intact. The night of D plus 3 was spent cruising the inlets and small islands west of the Bay of Cochinos looking for the Castro patrol boat *SV-3* which was reported captured by our people. No sign of this craft was found and at first light of D plus 4 we sailed into the Bay of Cochinos and up to the *Houston*. It was aground about 200 yards from shore and the decks were just above water. There was no sign of life and no trace of anyone ashore. We came out of the bay very close to the west shore and searched it with glasses but saw no one. We checked the lighthouse on the island of Cayo Piedras and found one of our 20 foot CEF boats drawn up on shore. We blew the ship's whistle repeatedly and went up and down both sides several times but found no sign of life. We then sailed to the west of the bay and started checking the keys that run off the

Fidel Castro on board a SUU-100 after the fighting.

swamps on the west side of the bay. On Cayo Blanco we spotted our first two survivors. The destroyer was about 800 yards from shore and the men ran out on the beach and started waving their shirts. We picked them up by sending the UDT team in to shore in the rubber boat using the 16hp silent motor. We then spotted other survivors and spent all day picking up small groups in the same manner. The destroyer then put its whale boat in the water to assist. Although these boats were forbidden to actually land on the beach they could transfer the survivors from the rubber boat and take them back to the ship leaving the UDT to continue their search. One UDT team of three men were put ashore and combed the islands all day to find the ones who could not or would not come

to the beach. Later in the day two Navy ADs [Skyraiders], propeller planes, were sent to us. They flew very low over the beaches and swamps and spotted several small groups. The UDT teams were then directed to these groups by radio and picked them up. The search was broken off at dark on D plus 4 and Mr. Lynch and three UDT men were transferred to the destroyer *Murray* which joined us that night. On D plus 5 the search was continued by both ships. The *Murray* was given the west side of the Bay of Cochinos down to the first islands and the *Eaton* and the *Conway* which also joined us that night had everything to the west. At first light on D plus 5, Mr. Lynch and three UDT men landed four miles south of the *Houston* and started to search for survivors. The coast was searched all the way to the islands but none found. We then started to comb the same keys as the day before and picked up several smaller groups. Due to physical exhaustion during this period, I cannot remember exact days. I believe we spent three or four days on this operation and were at one time or the other on four destroyers, one submarine and the aircraft carrier *Essex* twice. In all we picked up 26 survivors and found and buried one man on the beach. These survivors were in very bad condition and had been without food or water for five or six days. Most of them had only underwear or parts of uniforms left and some were naked. In all only two weapons were found among them, one pistol and one carbine. During this time three Castro helicopters were seen to the north of us flying very low over the swamps and were observed shooting the survivors by submachine [sic] guns from the air. They were seen to land on two occasions. One of these was a [two-man] helicopter and the other two large Russian types painted green with no markings.[68]

In fact, the later helicopters were the Bell 47s and Whirlwinds. The submarine named was the USS *Threadfin*, which also supported the search for survivors and gave protection in case any Cuban Navy ship attempted to attack the destroyers.

Also, on the 20th a whaler named *Cony* was used to rescue survivors and beached on a coral reef, where she was sighted by a FAR helicopter that fired upon the ship with a gun from a crew member, but Skyhawks from USS *Essex* forced the helicopter to leave. Finally, on 25 April, the rescue operations were finished and Task Force Alpha left the area and headed to Norfolk Naval Base.

Meanwhile, on 19 April, a group of 22 men, including Roberto Pérez San Román, commander of the Batallón 4 de Armas Pesadas and brother of the commander of the Brigade, and Alejandro del Valle, commander of Batallón 1, saw a 18ft-long fishing boat, the *Celia*, anchored about 100 metres from the coast and swam out to board it with the intention of using it to reach the US destroyers. As the engine was not working, they raised the sails and headed for the US ships, but the Americans did not see the fishing boat and sailed away at sunset. There were very little provisions of food and water, and when night fell, a strong wind took them far from the coast. Del Valle took command of the group and decided to head west, with the intention of reaching the Mexican coast. They sailed for many days, managing to capture some fish, but not enough for so many men. Without water and food, after a few days, one of the men, Vicente García, who was in charge of navigation thanks to his experience of sailing, died. He was the first of a total of 10 survivors who died on board the vessel, including Alejandro del Valle. After 15 days, they were rescued by the merchant ship *Atlanta Seaman* on 4 May, 100 miles to the south of the mouth of the Mississippi River. After they were rescued, two other survivors died on board the *Atlanta Seaman* and only 10 made it back

68 Grayston Lynch survey. National Defense University, Taylor Papers, Box 12, Cuba, Paramilitary Study. Secret; Eyes Only.

to tell their story.

Final air operations

A planned resupply operation using USAF C-130 Hercules was planned for the night of 19 April, but cancelled when the beach fell.

Also on 19 April, three C-46s and a C-54 tried to find and rescue the downed B-26 crews – but in vain. That evening, five C-46s were parked on the flight line at "Happy Valley". Also parked there that evening were four C-54s. One last C-54 mission was flown on 20 April, with Captain Eduardo Ferrer and his crew flying 10,000lb of supplies and weapons to the guerrillas in the Pinar del Río area, but when the C-54 arrived over the drop zone at about 10:00 p.m., it was greeted by anti-aircraft fire, so returned to base with its full load.

After the failure of the invasion, Connie Seigrist, Doug Price, Leo Turk (a CIA maintenance employee), some Air Guard personnel and a few CIA employees were assigned to stay on in Puerto Cabezas, as housekeepers for the Agency's property left behind. Seigrist recalled in his memoirs:

> Among our housekeeping duties we flew two C-46 flights loaded with boxes of undistributed propaganda leaflets to a safe distance from the coast out in the gulf away from sea traffic and dumped them into the sea. We also flew a few flights using B-26s to drop all the unused tanks of napalm on some exposed rocks a few miles out in the gulf. We participated in Civic Action assistance flying the C-46. A few flights were made to Managua for medical requirements or political purposes. We also delivered three B-26s to the Nicaraguan Air Force on the Managua airport. [At t]he end of July 1961 Capt. Price and I left Nicaragua ending our tour there.

The FAR's last operations in the area

On the morning of 20 April, Fernández and Del Pino received orders at San Antonio de los Baños to make a reconnaissance flight over the area of operations to check for enemy activity. They took off on the two available T-33s, serialled 709 and 711, and headed south-east. At Ensenada de los Cazones, about 15km to the west of Bay of Pigs, they saw the US destroyers *Eaton*, *Murray* and *Conway* with the boats that were rescuing men, as described by Grayston Lynch. Del Pino states he saw a total of five ships and thought that a huge landing by US forces had begun. He also saw two A-4B Skyhawks flying close by, so dived and flew as low as possible, and both T-33s returned to base.

Jacques Lagas also flew on a B-26 to Isla de Pinos and Bahía de Cochinos, seeing the US destroyers and some other vessels close to Cayo Guano, returning to base after that.

At 3:55 p.m., Del Pino and Fernández took off again on an identical mission, approaching very low to the Ensenada de los Cazones, where they made a steep climb to 1,500ft and saw four destroyers. They headed to Playa Larga, flying low over the ground, and then Fernández, on the 709, saw a pair of Skyhawks approaching, so the T-33s broke formation and returned to base.

Álvaro Prendes, with Douglas Rudd, also performed a reconnaissance mission during the day, between the two performed by the pair mentioned above, and another one after the last flight of Del Pino and Fernández, in which they saw a Skyhawk approaching them on their tails, but when they made a turn towards the plane, the Skyhawk climbed and left.

After these flights, the order was given to call a halt and keep the planes operational in case they were needed. The FAR knew they could do nothing if the US forces received the order to intervene directly in the actions, as the T-33s and Sea Furies were no match for the US planes.

CHAPTER 11
AFTERMATH

A total of 1,224 men of Brigade 2506 were captured from 19 April onwards, and all were taken to the Castillo del Príncipe in La Habana. Another nine died when more than 100 were taken in a closed truck for the long journey, dying of asphyxiation. On 6 September, 14 captured men were taken to Las Villas province to be judged for crimes committed during the Batista era, five of them being shot and nine sentenced to 30 years in prison, with two of those dying in jail. On 29 March 1962, a trial od the captured men was started, with sentencing on 7 April, each receiving either 30 years in prison or the payment of compensation to the Cuban government. The three commanders of the force (San Román, Oliva and Artime) were each to pay compensation of $500,000, 230 prisoners were to pay $100,000, 597 had to pay $50,000 and 371 $25,000. The 233 men facing the higher compensation charges were sent to the prison on Isla de Pinos.

The exiled Cuban community in the United States began actions to obtain the liberation of the imprisoned men, and on 14 April 1962, 60 men who were wounded in the invasion were freed and sent on a rented Pan American airplane to the Mercy Hospital in Miami.

Negotiations for the liberation of the remaining prisoners continued, with Castro asking for 500 large tractors - costing about $28 million - in exchange for them. On 21 December 1962, an agreement was signed between Castro and James B. Donovan, a US lawyer, for the exchange of 1,113 prisoners for $53 million, to be paid in agricultural equipment, food and medicines obtained from private donations.

Finally, on 23-24 December, all prisoners were sent to San Antonio de los Baños Air Base and then to the United States on board 14 chartered planes.

Officially, Castro said that 161 of the invaders had died, while the US government claimed the Brigade had killed more than 1,800 men. The two numbers seem highly unlikely, and most probably the actual number who died is between the two figures. The Brigade had 104 men killed, including the one killed in training and those who died on the boat that escaped from Girón and who died after being captured. Seventy-three died in combat, nine in the closed truck where they were being transported after being captured, five were executed in September 1961 and another five on 19 April 1961 after being captured. Twelve more died on the *Celia* after having escaped from Cuba.

As Kennedy's government decided to keep helping the Cubans in their fight against the Communist government of Castro, Dr Manuel Artime decided to present the president with the flag of the Brigade in a ceremony at Miami's Orange Bowl on 28 December 1962. Erneido Oliva and San Román handed the flag to the US president,

Discarded artillery ammunition boxes on the beaches of Girón.

Fidel Castro inspecting the wreckage of the plane of Matías Farías at Girón airfield.

Fidel Castro on the beach at Girón, shortly after the defeat of the Brigade.

Soldiers of the Milicias and the Cuban Army with one of the boats used by the Brigade during the landing.

José San Román, commander of the Brigade, after his capture.

Captured soldiers of the Brigade, with one wounded comrade.

Men of Brigada 2506 after being captured. The soldier of the Ejército Revolucionario is carrying a FAL rifle.

who declared that it would be returned to the Brigade "in a free La Habana". In the end, the promise was not kept and US support for the Cuban exiles eventually ceased.

Fidel Castro, despite the failure of the invasion, was sure that a new invasion would take place, or, more probably, a direct attack from the United States, so he immediately asked Soviet leader Nikita Khrushchev to increase his support for the island.

At the time of the invasion, the first 28 MiG-15 were already in crates in La Habana harbour, and entered San Antonio de los Baños Air Base on 6 June. Shortly after, with the first pilots trained in Czechoslovakia arriving at the base, the FAR obtained a respectable capacity to face any attempt to invade the island. In November 1961, Cuba also started to operate a squadron of MiG-19s, and in August 1962 the force received its first 36 MiG-21F-13s.

As Castro still feared a direct invasion by the United States, he asked for even more support from the USSR, including the deployment of ballistic missiles with nuclear warheads to the island. Khrushchev approved the request, and also deployed a squadron of Ilyushin Il-28 bombers and 30 launchers of SA-2 Guideline surface to air missiles. This lead to what was known as the Cuban Missile Crisis, which started on 22 October 1962, when the US convinced the Organization of American States to blockade Cuba to avoid any ship with Soviet ballistic missiles heading to the island. On 27 October, a Lockheed U-2F spy plane was shot down by a SA-2 and many RF-8 Crusaders on low-level reconnaissance missions were fired upon, but an agreement was finally reached by the US and Russian governments, under which the US would remove its missiles from Italy and Turkey, with the

Soviets doing the same with its missiles in Cuba, ending one of the most serious crises during the whole Cold War.

Despite many plans being made to overthrow Castro after the failure of Bay of Pigs, even to kill him, none of them were successful. As Soviet aid to Cuba increased, it became harder to envisage a military solution, as the Fuerzas Armadas Revolucionarias soon became very well trained and well equipped, forming a considerable force comprising more than 300,000 men. The guerrilla forces in the Escambray mountains, Pinar del Río and other areas of Cuba continued fighting, but with less and less success, especially after the end of the Missile Crisis when the US government decided to end any support for them, until by 1965 and early 1966 they had ceased to exist.

BIBLIOGRAPHY

Báez, Luis, *Secretos de Generales* (Barcelona: Editorial Losada, 1997).

Casaus, Victor, *Girón en la memoria* (La Habana: Editorial de Ciencias Sociales, 2001).

Castro Ruz, Fidel, *La Batalla de Girón* (La Habana: Cuban Government, 2011).

English, Adrian J., *Armed Forces of Latin America* (London: Jane's Publishing Company Ltd, 1984).

Fermoselle, Rafael, *The Evolution of the Cuban Military, 1492-1986* (Florida: Ediciones Universal, 1987).

Ferrer, Eduardo, *Operación Puma* (Florida: International Aviation Consultants, Inc., 1975).

Flintham, Victor, *Air Wars and Aircraft: A detailed record of air combat, 1945 to the present* (New York: Facts on File Inc., 1990).

Gaitan, Jose Ortega, *Los Paracaidistas* (Guatemala: Editorial Palo de Hormigo, 1997).

Hagedorn, Dan, *Central American and Caribbean Air Forces* (Shepperton: Air Britain, 1993).

Hagedorn, Dan, *Latin American Air Wars and Aircraft 1912-1969* (East Sussex, Hikoki, 2006).

Hagedorn, Dan, & Hellström, Leif, *Foreign Invaders* (Leicester: Midland Publishing, 1994).

Handbook on the Cuban Armed Forces (Washington DC: Defence Intelligence Agency, 1979).

Hawkins, Colonel J., *Record of paramilitary action against the Castro Government of Cuba, 5 May '61* (CIA doc. no. 0000132097).

Iglesias, Captain Manuel, & Caras, Captain Esteban Bovo, *La Historia de la Aviación Militar Cubana, 1913-1958* (Authors' edition, date unknown).

'Inspector General's Survey of the Cuban Operation', Central Intelligence Agency, October 1961.

Jones, Howard, *The Bay of Pigs* (New York: Oxford University Press, 2008).

Lagas, Jacques, *Memorias de un capitán rebelde* (Santiago de Chile: Editorial Del Pacífico 1964).

Leeker, Dr Joe F., 'Air America at the Bay of Pigs' (University of Texas, 4 March 2013).

Lynch, Grayston, *Decision for disaster: Betrayal at the Bay of Pigs* (Dulles, VA: Brassey's, 1998).

Meyer, Karl E., & Szulc, Tad, *The Cuban Invasion, The Chronicle of a Disaster* (New York: Frederic A. Praeger Publishers, 1962).

Persons, Albert C., *Bay of Pigs. A firsthand account of the mission by a U.S. pilot in support of the Cuban Invasion Force of 1961* (North Carolina: McFarland & Company, 1990).

Pfeiffer, Jack, *Official history of the Bay of Pigs Operation* (Central Intelligence Agency, 1979).

Pino, Rafael del, *Amanecer en Girón* (Cuba: Dirección Política de las FAR, 1969).

Pino, Rafael del, *9050 Horas* (Miami: CreateSpace, 2012).

Prendes, Álvaro, *En el punto rojo de mi kolimador. Crónicas de un aviador* (La Habana: Editorial Letras Cubanas, 1982).

Quesada, Alejandro de, *The Bay of Pigs, Cuba 1961* (Oxford: Osprey Publishing, 2009).

Rodriguez, Juan Carlos, *The Inevitable Battle, from the Bay of Pigs to Playa Girón* (La Habana: Editorial Capitán San Luis, 2009).

Rolas, Enrique Carreras, *Por el dominio del aire* (La Habana: Editora Política, 2008).

San Román, Comandante José Pérez, *Respuesta. La verdad sobre Girón* (Miami, Florida: Association of Veterans of the Bay of Pigs [Assault Brigade 2506] 1979).

Scheina, Robert L., *Latin America's Wars, Volume 2: The age of the professional soldier, 1900-2001* (Dulles, VA: Brassey's Inc., 2003).

Seigrist, Connie, *Memoirs* (University of Texas Dallas, William M. Leary Papers, Box 11 Folder 9).

Trest, Warren, & Dodd, Donald, *Wings of Denial. The Alabama Air National Guard's covert role at the Bay of Pigs* (Montgomery, Alabama: NewSouth Books, 2001).

Triay, Víctor Andrés, *Bay of Pigs. An oral history of Brigade 2506* (Gainesville, Florida: University Press of Florida, 2004).

Wyden, Peter, *Bay of Pigs, the Untold Story* (New York: Simon & Schuster, 1979).

ACKNOWLEDGEMENTS

The author wishes to thank the help he received from the following: General Rafael del Pino (Fuerza Aérea Revolucionaria), Jens Heidel, Gilles Hudicourt, Frank Resillez, Doug MacPhail, Amaru Tincopa, Layo Leiva, Mario Overall, Helio Higúchi, Colonel Mario Grajeda (Guatemalan Army), Colonel Jorge Antonio Ortega Gaitán (Guatemalan Army), Carmina Valdizán, Luis Roberto Córdova Sáenz and Dan Hagedorn.

ABOUT THE AUTHOR

Santiago Rivas was born in Buenos Aires, Argentina in 1977. Twenty years later, the Journalism graduate started to work in the fields of aviation and defence journalism – travelling all across Latin America to conduct his research for articles and books. In 2007 he published his first book, which was about the Malvinas/Falklands War, for a Brazilian publisher – and since then, another 12 have been published across the globe in Argentina, Brazil, France, Germany and the United Kingdom, while four more are soon to be released. He has also had articles published in more than 50 magazines in 20 countries – and he currently works for more than 20 of the magazines. Santiago has three children and lives in Buenos Aires. He continues to travel every year to most of the Latin American countries to fulfil his research-based work.